THE GREY

WIDOW-MAKER

BERNARD EDWARDS

The true stories of
twenty-four disasters at sea

Futura

A *Futura* Book

First published in Great Britain in 1990 by Robert Hale Limited
First published in paperback by Futura Publications 1992
This edition published by Futura Publications 1995

ISBN 0 7088 5241 6

Printed in England by Clays Ltd, St Ives plc

Futura Publications
A Division of
Macdonald & Co (Publishers)
Brettenham House
Lancaster Place
London WC2E 7EN

Contents

For

Susannah

What is a woman that you forsake her,
And the hearth-fire and the home acre,
To go with the old grey Widow-maker?

She has no house to lay a guest in –
But one chill bed for all to rest in,
That the pale suns and the stray bergs nest in.

Rudyard Kipling, 'Harp Song of the Dane Women'

Illustrations

PICTURE CREDITS

National Maritime Museum: 1, 2, 3. A. Duncan: 4. *Western Mail*: 5, 6, 9. *Wellington Evening Post*: 7. *Guernsey Evening Press*: 10. Times Newspapers: 11. *Sunday Express*: 12.

Preface

A long, lazy voyage across the Indian Ocean in the north-east monsoon offers the ultimate in sheer tranquillity. Day after day of cloudless blue skies, warm tropical nights under a star-studded mantle of deepest sable, and all the while the sea a gently undulating mirror of shimmering cobalt. Gone are the petty irritations and complications of the shore. Life takes on a timeless serenity, paced by the coming and going of the sun and moon and interrupted only by the swish of the bow wave and the snort of the playful dolphin.

In contrast, the perpetually angry North Atlantic, with its cacophony of howling winds and rampaging seas, provides an adrenalin-booster without comparison. Yet it is well to remember that the power of the sea is absolute. No man who has ever challenged the 'grey widow-maker' on a day-to-day basis will refute this. He will tell you that the sea, in its darker moods, is sly, vindictive and brutal; an adversary never to be underrated or ignored.

This book follows the changing pattern of man's fortunes at sea, from the golden age of sail, through the proud years when steam reigned supreme, to the present day, when the flag of convenience rules the waves. It tells of triumphs and disasters, some recent, some long forgotten, and illustrates how, contrary to expectations, the fine art of seamanship has withered and died with the advent of high technology.

One hundred and fifty years ago, seafaring was a high-risk occupation second to none, and for good reasons. Sailing-ships, often overloaded, steering by unreliable compasses and subject to the vagaries of the wind, put to sea and disappeared with all hands as regularly as the sun rose and set. Few seamen of the 1800s lived to rest their bones beneath the sod of their native land.

Today, those who go down to the sea in ships should do so in comparative safety. Modern ships are large and powerfully engined and carry navigational equipment capable of accurate position-fixing in all weathers. Radio communication with the remotest shores and other ships is clear and instantaneous. Yet accidents at sea have become ever more bizarre and destructive as the new flag-of-convenience sailors, dazzled by electronics and blinkered by ignorance, contemptuously present their backs to the 'grey widow-maker'. Their watery graves lie scattered over the oceans, from the China Sea to the South Atlantic, from the Pacific to the Mediterranean.

1   The Hard Road to Botany Bay

On 29 April 1770 Captain James Cook, fresh from his circumnavigation of New Zealand, took his ship, the 370-ton barque HMS *Endeavour*, into an unexplored bay on the south-west coast of Australia. As the bay was sheltered from the great Pacific rollers and appeared green and pleasant, Cook marked it down as a place for a possible settlement and took possession in the name of the British Crown. Eight years later, when Cook met his untimely end at the hands of a band of irate Hawaiian islanders, Botany Bay, named for its profusion of unusual plants, was still untouched by the colonist's axe. It was perhaps just as well that Cook did not live to see the humiliation heaped upon his discovery in later years.

The uprising of the American colonists and the final defeat of British forces at Yorktown in 1781 did more than wound British pride; it caused a major upset in the penal system of the Mother Country. Hitherto, it had been the custom of the British courts to banish undesirable offenders to the Americas, thus relieving the pressure on the gaols at home and at the same time providing cheap labour for the sparsely populated colony. American independence put a stop to this convenient practice and forced the British government to look elsewhere for a dumping-ground for the country's unruly elements. Captain Cook's report on his exploration of the coast of New South Wales was taken down from the shelf on which it had been gathering dust, and the potential of Botany Bay was re-examined. The colonization of Australia was about to begin.

The fleet which assembled in Portsmouth harbour in May 1787 was not an inspiring sight. The ships were a poor lot, as were their passengers. The 600-ton flagship *Sirius* was a cast-off from the Honourable East India Company, parsimoniously refitted, armed with twenty guns and taken into the king's service for the occasion. Her consort, the tiny 170-ton *Supply*, should not really have contemplated venturing beyond the limits of the English Channel. In their charge, these two third-rate men-of-war had the transports *Alexander*, *Scarborough*, *Friendship*, *Prince of Wales*, *Charlotte* and *Lady Penrhyn*, a string of 300-tonners noted for their leaky hulls and poor sailing qualities. Completing this mediocre assembly were the small supply ships *Fishbourne*, *Golden Grove* and one other whose name has disappeared into the mists of time. The First Fleet, as it was to become known, carried a total of 1,350 souls, made up of 570 seamen and marines and 780 convicts in irons. The latter, men, women and children, were to be the first colonists of Australia, their destination Botany Bay.

Unfortunately there were no journalists on hand to record the feelings of the poor wretches as they were herded aboard the superannuated transports to face months of hardship and deprivation on the high seas. They were a pathetic crowd, petty criminals mostly: sheep-stealers, prostitutes, child pickpockets, many of them victims of the Industrial Revolution attracted to the towns, where the living was hard and the temptations were legion. However, such were the horrors they had already endured at the hands of His Majesty's gaolers that it is most likely they felt they had little to lose except their lives. Given the state of the ships and the perils of the voyage ahead, the latter seemed a distinct possibility.

The First Fleet set out on the first leg of its voyage, bound for Tenerife in the Canaries, on 13 May, five months later than planned. In command, and sailing in the *Sirius*, was Captain Arthur Phillip, a proven navigator, an honest and compassionate man. From the outset, he was determined to alleviate the sufferings of his convict passengers by all means in his power. His orders to the captains of the transports were that strict attention be paid to cleanliness and that convicts be given as much fresh air and exercise as was commensurate with good order. He further instructed that the women be kept separate from the men and that food and water be fairly shared amongst all, convict and crew alike. As to offences committed on board ship during the voyage, Phillip made it quite clear that the responsibility for the judgment and punishment of major crimes should remain in his hands. There were those in the fleet, particularly Major Ross, commandant of marines, and Captain Meridith of the *Friendship*, who regarded Phillip as being too lenient and were determined to handle things their way.

Despite Arthur Phillip's good intentions, there were difficulties right from the start. It had been agreed to issue all convicts with proper clothing before boarding the ships but, owing to the incompetence or corruption of those ashore, most of the prisoners arrived as they had left their cells, half-naked and filthy. It was all Phillip could do to find enough clothes in the ships to cover the women. Before the fleet cleared the Channel, fever had broken out in the *Lady Penrhyn*, probably as a result of exposure. Aboard the *Friendship* there was trouble of a different kind, when her crew demanded extra meat rations. The crew of the *Scarborough* joined in the action, and Phillip was obliged to act harshly and swiftly to prevent the mutiny's spreading throughout the fleet. Land's End was not yet out of sight astern when, on the 15th, Corporal Baker of the marines accidentally shot himself in the foot, the ball from his musket then ricocheting off a cask of salt beef to kill two precious geese long before their time had come. This was hardly an auspicious beginning to a voyage destined to last eight months.

Once clear of the Channel, it was a long, hard slog westwards, battling against the prevailing winds and blustery spring gales, until the longitude of 12° west was reached. The fleet then came round onto a south-westerly course to run across the mouth of the Bay of Biscay, with the wind on the starboard beam. In the long Atlantic swell the small ships rolled heavily and without let-up. Seasickness is a miserable and debilitating affliction at the best of times; aggravated by overcrowding and lack of sanitation, it made life a living hell for the convicts.

A week out of Portsmouth and with Cape Finisterre astern, the ships came under the influence of the Portuguese trade winds, fresh north-easterlies, before which they could run as steady as any small sailing-ship can ever be. The reduced motion, combined with the warmer air, eased the suffering of the miserable wretches below decks. But the improvement came too late for one of their number. On 28 May Ishmael Coleman, unable to endure any more, gave up the struggle and died. On that same day John Bennet, described as 'a young man but an old rogue', broke free of his chains and received eighty-seven lashes for his efforts. But it was not all gloom. Three days later, when passing Madeira, Isabella Lawson, transported for stealing from her employer, gave birth to a baby girl. Not to be outdone, the *Sirius*'s goat produced two healthy kids.

It was with some relief that, after twenty days at sea, the island of Tenerife was reached on 2 June. Here the fleet rested for a week and took on fresh provisions and water. The convicts were not allowed ashore, but at least they were free of the interminable rolling that had made their lives such a misery at sea. Green figs, onions and pumpkin added to their monotonous diet of salt beef, and hard tack also gave a much-needed boost to their morale.

Having tasted the delights of the Canaries, the fleet sailed for the South Atlantic on 9 June. The north-east trades were blowing strong and, with the wind right astern, the ships made good speed. But as they moved into the tropics, the weather became hot and humid. The female convicts, who, largely for their own safety, Phillip had ordered to be battened down below decks at night, suffered terribly in their airless, floating dungeons. As a passage of at least fifty days lay ahead of them, Phillip wisely rationed the fresh water from the start. Each man and woman, whether convict or crew, was allowed three pints a day for washing and drinking. Personal hygiene became an irrelevance, and in the *Alexander*, whose master paid little attention to cleanliness, a fever broke out which threatened to engulf the whole fleet.

South of the Cape Verde Islands, the trades petered out, and the agony was increased as the ships drifted into the Doldrums, that broad band of light winds and calms cursed by sailing-ships down through the ages. Sails were constantly tended to catch every fitful breath of wind, but for the most part the ships wallowed helplessly in the long swell, and it seemed to those on board that they were doomed to wander forever in this windless sea. The sun was almost overhead and shone down from a cloudless sky with no mercy for captor or captive. Inevitably water began to run short, and Phillip was forced to cut the ration. Thirst was added to all the miseries already being suffered.

At last the Equator was crossed, and then came the first of the south-east trades. Within a few days these blew with unexpected ferocity, but they were fair winds, bringing the blessed rain with them. Cramming on all possible sail, the ships surged southwards at a cracking pace, their lee gunwales awash. The miles were eaten up, but there was a price to pay for progress: the *Sirius* lost a topmast, one seaman went overboard to his death, and a woman convict was killed when a ship's boat broke loose and crushed her.

Brazil's fine natural harbour of Rio de Janeiro, the largest of its kind in the world, was entered on 1 August after fifty-three days at sea. In this sun-drenched land of plenty, while the ships were repaired and reprovisioned, Phillip and his officers were lavishly entertained by the ruling Portuguese. So taken were they by the delights of Rio that the fleet languished in the harbour for five weeks. As far as the convicts were concerned, apart from the lack of rolling and the blessing of fresh vegetables, they might just as well have been at sea. They were confined to the transports under guard and had no contact with the shore. The fleet chaplain, Richard Johnson, possibly for the want of something better to do, visited each ship in turn to preach to the captive congregations. It is unlikely that his ministrations were much appreciated.

The fleet finally left Rio on 5 September and set course east by south for Cape Town. The ships were now well stocked with fresh fruit and vegetables, and all on board, including the convicts, had benefited from the long, idle days in port. But the euphoria generated by this pleasant sojourn was quickly dispelled when, two days after leaving port, a series of gales began which was to last almost without interruption for the whole of the 3,400-mile passage. Yet another man was lost overboard, dysentery reared its ugly head, and there was open mutiny in the crew of the *Alexander*, whose master had by now proved himself to be thoroughly incompetent. Because of the foul weather, the convicts were kept below decks most of the time, resulting in a great deal of unrest in their ranks. There was an inevitable increase in the daily punishment round. The future citizens of Botany Bay had come to wish they had never left the comparative comfort of the Crown lodging-houses.

There was still worse to come. When the bedraggled fleet anchored in the shadow of Table Mountain on 13 October, it received a chilly welcome from the Dutch colonists, who were not on the best of terms with the British. At first, the governor of Cape Town refused point-blank to supply provisions. However, Phillip, having no other choice, refused to sail until his ships were restocked. The governor relented, but the prices charged for the supplies were three times the normal. Some of the ships had been severely damaged in the bad weather of the South Atlantic, and the necessary repairs took almost a month. It was 12 November, with relations between the Dutch and British stretched to breaking-point, before the fleet finally bade a sailor's farewell to the Cape.

Now came the real test of the voyage, the 7,000-mile leg across the bottom of the world to the Antipodes. The fleet was obliged first to steer well south into the Roaring Forties in order to make maximum progress eastwards. Here, on the edge of the great Southern Ocean, where the malevolent westerlies blow without let or hindrance right around the world, and giant icebergs drift shrouded in fog, was the final proving-ground for the aspiring colonists. As it was, conditions in the ships were already worse than they had been at any time in the voyage. With the needs of the new colony in mind, Phillip had shipped a large quantity of livestock in Cape Town. If the transports had been crowded before, they were now bursting at the seams. Pigs, horses, cows, sheep, bales of fodder and extra barrels of water filled every available inch of deck space. Running before storm-force winds and angry, tumbling seas, the tiny ships of the First Fleet were like paper boats carried along on a mountain torrent. With sickening regularity they were pooped, swamped or laid on their beam ends. There was not a dry spot anywhere, above or below decks. Animals and men were washed overboard or drowned where they slept; others just died of sheer exhaustion from the incessant pummelling they received at the hands of the elements. Christmas Day came and went unnoticed, except for a special grog issue for the hard-pressed seamen – the convicts were past caring. Three days later, the situation worsened – if such a thing was conceivably possible – when the dreaded scurvy made its appearance. The first day of 1788, ushered in at the height of a storm of demoniacal proportions, found the fleet 800 miles from Botany Bay and running short of food, water and fuel for the galley fires.

On 7 January 1788, fifty-six days out of Table Bay, came the first sight of land, when the southern tip of Tasmania – or Van Diemen's Land as it was then known – came over the horizon. Eleven days later, after weathering more gales and a spell of dense fog, the battered fleet entered Botany Bay, only to find it, contrary to Captain Cook's glowing report, a barren place totally unsuited for a permanent settlement. Another eight days were to elapse before a boat party discovered a magnificent deep-water harbour a few miles to the north, in which, in Captain Arthur Phillip's words, 'a thousand sail of the line may ride in the most perfect security'. The ships moved into Port Jackson – so named from afar by Cook – and the birth of Australia became a reality.

The voyage of the First Fleet from Portsmouth to Botany Bay had taken eight months and one week. Of the 1,350 souls who set out in the ships, forty had died on the way. That the fleet reached Australia at all was a great tribute to the navigational prowess, professionalism and tenacity of Captain Arthur Phillip, who was to become the first governor of the new colony of New South Wales.

2 The East Indiaman

When Persian armies led by Nadir Shah swept into northern India in 1739, they captured and ransacked the ancient palace of the Moguls in Delhi, stripping the building clean of all its fabulous wealth. Among their plunder was the magnificent Peacock Throne, on which the Mogul emperors had sat. The throne, shaped like a bed, was moulded in solid gold, encrusted with diamonds, emeralds and rubies and backed by two golden peacocks, also lavishly studded with precious stones, from which it took its name. This was treasure on which no man could put a value. Nadir Shah took the throne back to Persia, where it then disappeared from view. It is thought it may have been broken up and distributed amongst the shah's followers, but whatever happened to the Peacock Throne, it was never to be seen again. The two golden peacocks, on the other hand, said to be worth a vast fortune on their own, came to light forty-three years later, when, securely packed in an iron-studded chest, they were loaded aboard the Eastern Indiaman *Grosvenor*, bound for Britain. Where the peacocks had lain hidden all those years, and who acquired them, is to this day still a mystery.

For the Honourable East India Company, the year 1782 was not a happy one. In the first half of the year no fewer than five of its ships were lost. Of these, three were on their maiden voyages: the *Fortitude* taken by pirates off the Coromandel Coast, the *Earl of Dartmouth* wrecked on the Nicobar Islands, and the *Major* destroyed by fire on the Ganges. The company was rich and could withstand such losses comfortably, but when news was received in November of that year that the *Grosvenor* was overdue and believed lost with all hands at sea, there was consternation in London.

The *Grosvenor*, 729 tons, commanded by Captain John

Coxon, sailed from Trincomalee, on Ceylon's east coast, on 13 June 1782, bound for London. She was a well-found ship, with a highly trained crew and armed with twenty-eight 18-pounder guns. Her total complement of 135 passengers and crew included eighty Europeans, mostly British. Her cargo, apart from the usual Indian produce, included gold, precious stones and ivory to the value of £2 million. In her strong-room, a secret shared only by Captain Coxon and his chief officer, was a consignment worth more than the *Grosvenor* and her cargo put together. The golden peacocks of the Moguls were on their way to a new home.

Ahead of the *Grosvenor* lay a voyage of 11,000 miles, a voyage beset with many dangers. Foul weather, marauding pirates and patrolling Dutch men-of-war – Britain was at that time engaged in a bitter war with the Netherlands – all lay in her path. But for the East Indiaman's passengers and crew, perhaps the greatest hardship to come was to be cooped up in this tiny ship (she was no more than 160 feet by thirty-four feet) for seven long months. Because of the war with the Dutch, there could be no call at Cape Town to reprovision, so it would be necessary strictly to ration food and water. Sanitation, of course, would be of the most rudimentary, and for the unfortunate passengers, many of them women and children, there would be the awful, morale-destroying curse of seasickness. This was to be a voyage of endurance, but there was not one on board who doubted that it would be completed.

The passage south across the Indian Ocean could not have been worse. The south-west monsoon was at its height, and from the time of sailing from Trincomalee until she neared the Equator, the *Grosvenor* battled against adverse gale-force winds and heavy seas. There followed day after day lolling in the calms of the Doldrums under a blazing sun that melted the pitch in her deck seams and turned her accommodation into a living hell before, at last, the south-east trades began to fill her sails. But the belated progress she then made was short-lived. South of Madagascar, the *Grosvenor* ran into the first of the south-westerly gales that ravage the South African coast in winter. The battle against the elements was resumed.

On 3 August the ship was fifty-one days on passage and in a position estimated to be some 700 miles east of the Cape of Good Hope. The skies had been overcast for two days past, and it had not been possible to take sights to verify this position, but Captain Coxon was confident enough of his reckoning to assure his guests at dinner that night that all was well. The ship, he maintained, was at least a hundred miles off the land and would pass well south of the cape as she sailed to the west.

Yet another gale blew up during the night, and the *Grosvenor* was forced to heave to under shortened sail. At about two o'clock on the morning of the 4th, in a break in the rain, Second Officer Shaw, who had the watch on deck, sighted a flickering light right ahead. He was about to put this down to another ship on the same course when he saw first one, then two, then a line of dancing lights stretching right across the bow. Shaw had seen native fires on a darkened coastline many times before, and it seemed to him that, even though she should have been many miles from the land, the *Grosvenor* was about to run ashore. Without hesitation and praying he was not too late, Shaw called all hands and began to put the ship about.

The shrilling of bosun's pipes and the stamp of hurrying feet brought Captain Coxon on deck. By this time, the rain had closed in again and the lights were no longer visible. Shaw tried to explain his fears, but Coxon would have none of it. As far as he was concerned, the ship was well clear of the land. He ordered Shaw to resume course and then retired to his cabin again.

Having, albeit reluctantly, put the ship back on her original course, Shaw resumed his pacing of the poop, trying hard to convince himself that the lights had been a figment of his overwrought imagination. It was a black and heavily overcast night, certainly a night on which a man's eyes might play strange tricks. The watch dragged on and the fears Shaw had harboured began to fade. Then, as one bell was struck to signify the last quarter-hour of the watch, there was a frenzied shout from the lookout aloft: 'Breakers ahead!'

And so began the long nightmare. Coxon was called on deck and attempted to wear ship, but it was too late. Carried on the back of a huge, tumbling swell, her sails hanging limp, the *Grosvenor* was hurled ashore, the terrible grinding of her timbers on the rocks matched by the screaming of her passengers.

Held fast by rocks that had pierced her bottom, and pounded by the angry waves, the East Indiaman began to break up within a short time of grounding. Distress signals were fired but,

although the ship appeared to be not more than 300 yards from
the shore, no answer came. Coxon ordered that the pumps be
started and the masts cut away, hoping this would lighten the
ship and she would float off. Again the result was disappointing.
The *Grosvenor*, cast up on an unknown and probably
uninhabited shore, was doomed.

Coxon now turned to the problem of saving his passengers
and crew. The ship's two boats were lowered, but they were
immediately dashed to pieces against the ship's side, fortunately
without loss of life. A raft was then constructed, with the idea of
floating a hawser ashore. This time the launching was
successful, but the raft disintegrated in the raging surf just a few
yards from the ship. Three men lost their lives. Three others,
who were powerful swimmers, volunteered to swim ashore with
a line. It was a fearful risk, but two of the three men reached the
shore, the other being lost in the surf.

When the swimmers landed, they were surrounded by a
crowd of natives, who appeared to be friendly. With their help, a
heavier line was hauled ashore from the *Grosvenor* and made fast
to a rock. A few minutes later the stricken ship broke in two, but
the hawser held. Some men reached the shore hand-over-hand
on the hawser, but fifteen fell to their deaths in the surf while
attempting this perilous route.

The shock of seeing so many men lost put an end to all efforts
to escape. Those left on board huddled together on the poop,
awaiting their fate, for they were sure the ship would not last
until dawn. Then, miraculously it seemed, the stern half of the
ship broke clear of the rocks holding it and drifted into shallow
and sheltered water close to the shore. All 115 on board reached
the safety of dry land.

Most of the survivors were in a pitiful condition when they
landed. Wet, frightened and exhausted by their ordeal, they had
no idea of where they had come ashore. Of one thing they were
certain: it was a wild and forbidding place. The rocky beach was
backed by sand dunes, and beyond that, some three miles
inland, stood a wall of dense, impenetrable forest. They were, in
fact, in Pondoland, about a hundred miles south-west of what is
now called Durban and near the mouth of the Lombazi river.
But this was then largely unexplored country, and they had no
means of identifying their location. The Kaffirs, of course,
spoke a language which was unintelligible to all, so they were of

little help. Furthermore, they seemed to be showing an unhealthy interest in the few possessions the survivors had managed to bring ashore. Coxon decided it would be wise to move on as soon as possible. He knew that somewhere to the west lay the Dutch colony of the Cape, but he had no idea how far it was to the nearest settlement. It might be five days' march, or it might be fifteen; certainly the going would be hard.

Having collected some casks of provisions and tools washed ashore from the wreck, the survivors spent the remainder of the night around a fire built on the beach by the Kaffirs. It must have occurred, with some irony, to both Coxon and Shaw that they were probably sitting close to one of the fires the second officer had seen two hours before the *Grosvenor* struck.

When daylight came, Coxon sent men to scour the beach for anything else that might have come ashore, then the whole party set off to the west, carrying one of their number who had been injured in the wreck. They had not gone far before the Kaffirs began to follow them in large numbers. At first the natives kept their distance, although they had become decidedly unfriendly. As the day wore on, they grew bolder and moved in, first to touch and then to steal the few possessions the *Grosvenor*'s survivors had. None of Coxon's party was armed, so they could do little to deter their unwelcome escorts.

For several days the band of survivors struggled westwards along the inhospitable coast, keeping the foraging Kaffirs at bay by buying them off with trinkets and, when these ran out, by confrontation that stopped just short of violence. The hostile band surrounding them was swelling all the time, and Coxon, conscious that he had women and children with him, wished to avoid a fight at all costs. Their route was intersected by numerous rivers, and wild beasts roamed the edge of the forest, adding to the dangers they already faced. The women and children began to tire, slowing the progress of the party to a mere crawl.

Day followed day, and soon all food was exhausted and the survivors were reduced to living off shellfish and roots. The Kaffirs stole their only tinderbox, and they were obliged to carry their fire with them in the form of burning torches. Many collapsed through malnutrition and exhaustion, others simply did not have the will to carry on. Eventually it was decided that forty-three of the fittest men would go on ahead to find a

settlement and bring help. Coxon and his officers stayed with the
sick, the women and children, planning to strike north into the
forest and there make camp, secure, it was hoped, from the
increasingly hostile Kaffirs.

Four months later seven emaciated, half-crazed men walked
into a Dutch farm in the Cape colony. They were the only
survivors of the forty-three who had set out to find civilization.
The rest had died on the long trek, succumbing to hunger, thirst,
wild beasts or the Kaffirs. Although the Dutch were at war with
Britain, when the governor of the colony heard of the arrival of the
seven men, he sent out an expedition several hundred strong to
search for Coxon and the others. Another three months passed
and the search party returned with twelve more pitiful wretches,
three white men, seven Lascars and two Indian ayahs. Of the
remaining sixty, no trace could be found. To this day, their fate is
unknown, but many years after the loss of the *Grosvenor* there
were reports of a strange tribe of light-skinned Kaffirs in the area
where she came ashore. It could be that some of the white women
survived and were taken into the native kraals.

The *Grosvenor*, her rotting hulk now buried deep in the sands,
still lies thirty yards off the shore near Port Grosvenor, to which
she gave her name. Numerous attempts have been made to
salvage her fabulous treasure, but this is a dangerous coast,
fringed by jagged rocks and pounded by surf. A few guns, a
handful of gold coins and odd items of personal effects have been
recovered, but none of the gold bars, precious stones and ivory
the ship was said to be carrying. As to the fabulous peacocks of the
Moguls, they are lost forever – or at least until man's technology is
equal to the might of the sea.

The East India Company's run of bad luck continued long after
the *Grosvenor* went ashore. At the end of August that same year,
the 703-ton *Brilliant* was lost on the Comoro Islands, and then in
October yet another ship on her maiden voyage, the 758-ton *Earl
of Hertford*, was sunk in a violent storm while alongside the quay in
Madras. The year following, 1783, proved even more disastrous,
the company losing six more valuable ships, including the *Duke of
Kingston*, which caught fire off Ceylon with the loss of sixty-five
lives. There were those who murmured about the curse of the
Moguls being on the company. Perhaps they were right.

3   A Dog's Chance

In a forgotten corner of the Hull Museum of Fisheries and Shipping stands the carved wooden figure of a mongrel dog, weathered by the sea and blackened by age. The dog's outstretched paws once offered up a symbolic star, but this star is long gone, lost in the mists of time like the memory of the ship this quaint figurehead adorned; a ship which, accidentally caught up in the events of her day, inaugurated a golden age at sea that was to last for 120 years.

At the beginning of the nineteenth century, the vigorous new world of North America was poised to unleash its unprecedented brand of innovation and enterprise on the world. Much of the wealth and expertise to feed this bubbling revolution lay in Britain, and passenger traffic back and forth across the North Atlantic was booming. However, the habitually stormy passage was hazardous, uncomfortable and, above all, dreadfully slow. Even the fastest sailing-packets took up to thirty days, the slower ones twice as long. For the entrepreneur in a hurry, the North Atlantic crossing was a dreary, nail-biting ordeal. The steam-engine, which had been in use in coastal and river vessels for forty years, seemed the obvious answer to the dilemma but it was, as yet, notoriously unreliable. Atlantic crossings had been made with steam assisting sail, but never under steam alone.

Junius Smith, an American trader living in London and a frequent commuter across the Atlantic, was one who had faith in steam. He was also acutely aware of the benefits a fast, reliable transatlantic service could bring. With the help of British money, Smith established the British & American Steam Navigation Company in 1836, and the keel of the company's first ship was laid in Macgregor Laird's Birkenhead yard that year. The *Royal Victoria*, a paddle-steamer of 1,890 tons gross, was to be the largest and most luxurious steamer afloat, a fitting contender for the title of 'first across the Atlantic under steam only'.

Not to be outdone, the restless genius Isambard Kingdom Brunel hastened to fulfil his dream of joining London to New York via the Great Western Railway and the port of Bristol. Funded by a group of West Country businessmen, the Great Western Steamship Company was set up and Brunel saw his brainchild, the *Great Western*, begin to take form on the stocks of a Bristol shipyard. The race was on.

Junius Smith's American-inspired venture was the first to suffer a major setback. The Glasgow company building the *Royal Victoria*'s engines went bankrupt, and Smith was left with a powerless hull on his hands at a time when Brunel's *Great Western* was nearing completion. Smith might have dropped the matter there and then, but what had begun as a friendly challenge had now developed into a much-looked-forward-to event involving considerable national pride. Smith was synonymous with America, Brunel with Britain, and large wagers on the outcome of the race were being laid on both sides of the Atlantic. Smith was obliged to find a substitute vessel to carry the flag of the British & American Steam Navigation Company.

The honour fell to the paddle-steamer *Sirius*, owned by the St George Steam Packet Company of Cork. Built in 1837 by Menzies of Leith, the 703-ton *Sirius* had hitherto been engaged exclusively in the coastal trade between Cork and London, her keel never having kissed the deep waters. She was a two-master with a tall funnel and, at 208 feet long and only twenty-five feet in the beam, she had a sleek look that was somewhat spoiled by the drabness of her green and black paintwork. Her engines developed a horsepower of 320, giving her, in fine weather, a speed of eight knots on twenty-four tons of coal a day. Like all steamers of her day, she carried a full set of sails. Her only distinguishing feature was a figurehead in the shape of a dog holding a star in its paws, representing the dog star Sirius.

In comparison, Brunel's purpose-built transatlantic steamer was huge. Of 1,320 tons gross, the four-masted *Great Western* had an overall length of 236 feet and a beam of thirty-five feet. Luxury cabin accommodation was provided for 128 passengers, with a rather less luxurious twenty-berth dormitory for servants. Her great saloon, seventy-five feet long, twenty-one feet wide and nine feet high, was said to be the most lavishly appointed ever seen in a passenger ship. Below decks, more than half the space was taken up by two massive side-lever engines developing a horsepower of 750, four iron boilers and vast coal bunkers capable of holding 800 tons.

At the end of March 1838 both ships were in the London river being fussed over like high-bred racehorses. The passenger accommodation aboard the *Sirius*, previously somewhat spartan, had been gutted and refurbished in a much grander style, and an extra cabin had been built on her after deck. Yet, for all the refinements, she was still basically a coastal paddle-steamer, and the odds being offered against her being first across the Atlantic under steam only were high. On 28 March the two ships set off down the Thames, the *Great Western* to call at Bristol and the *Sirius* at Cork to embark passengers.

The *Great Western* commanded by Captain James Hosken, ran into trouble even before she had cleared the river. Her boiler lagging caught fire, and serious damage to her engines was only narrowly averted. In the confusion Brunel, who was on board for the passage to Bristol, fell eighteen feet into the engine-room and was badly injured. Captain Hosken had little option but to beach his ship off Southend, so that the fire could be extinguished and Brunel landed into hospital. The *Great Western* was floated off on the next high tide, but by this time the *Sirius*, her red-painted paddlewheels threshing the water determinedly, had a good twelve-hour lead.

When the *Sirius* arrived at Cork, Captain Richard Roberts, a local man, was appointed to command, and no time was lost in preparing the little ship for her first ocean passage. Moored alongside Penrose Quay in the shadow of her owner's head office, she took on 454 tons of bunker coal, twenty tons of fresh water, a cargo of fifty-eight casks of resin, and forty passengers and their baggage. It was just as well the introduction of the Plimsoll Line was some years away, for the *Sirius* was dangerously overloaded. Doubtless her passengers would have missed the significance of this, for the excitement was high, with thousands of well-wishers lining the shore to see the ship off. At ten o'clock on the morning of 4 April a gun was fired and the *Sirius* pulled away from the quay, her tall funnel belching black smoke and her flags snapping in the breeze. Ahead of her lay 2,897 miles of the most inhospitable ocean of all.

In Ireland that year it was as though winter would never end. Although spring flowers bloomed timorously in the hedgerows, the sky remained stubbornly overcast and the rain had an icy lash to it. The North Atlantic, beset by an unending procession of vigorous depressions, had been in a constant state of agitation for months. When the *Sirius* left the shelter of Cork harbour, she steamed straight into the mouth of Hell itself.

Captain Roberts, ever conscious of the spectre of the larger and more powerful *Great Western* lurking somewhere astern, did not flinch. He ordered his chief engineer to work his engines up to maximum revolutions and to keep them that way at all costs. The *Sirius* was soon burying her canine figurehead deep as she met and breasted the mountainous waves of the open Atlantic. In her stokehold, fighting to keep their feet on the heaving plates, gangs of sweating firemen bent their backs to hurl ton after ton of coal into her roaring furnaces.

If things were bad for the little steamer's hard-bitten firemen, they were even worse for her passengers battened down in the airless accommodation. Tossed from side to side by the violent motion of the ship, deafened by the awful cacophony of clanging pistons, hissing steam and thumping paddle-blades, they suffered the horrors of confusion, seasickness and abject fear.

On the afternoon of the 7th, the *Sirius* was sighted by an inbound clipper 433 miles to the west of Cork, having, in spite of the fearful weather, averaged just over six knots since leaving port. Dick Roberts, deaf to the pleadings of his passengers and the increasingly ominous rumblings amongst his crew, would conquer the Atlantic or drive his ship under in the attempt.

Although he was not aware of the fact, Roberts was wise to push his ship, for the very next morning the *Great Western*, having repaired her fire damage, came thundering out of Bristol hell-bent on making up lost time. She carried in her splendid 128-berth accommodation only seven passengers, the rest having cried off after the accident in the Thames. As a commercial venture, the maiden voyage of the *Great Western* was doomed, and Captain Hosken's professional reputation was at stake. Only a record crossing and arrival ahead of the *Sirius* would save the day for both.

Meanwhile, deep in the Atlantic, the *Sirius*, lighter by more than a hundred tons of coal, continued to ride the seas successfully, but Roberts had a crisis on his hands. Terrified by the huge and unfamiliar waves, some of the crew of the steamer had mutinied and were demanding that Roberts turn back for Ireland. The mutiny was short-lived, for Roberts, like many a sailing-ship master before him, simply gathered his officers around him and drove the men back to their posts at gunpoint.

On the 12th, in mid-ocean, the *Sirius* ran into problems of another kind. After eight days of hard steaming through the stormy seas, a number of paddle-blades had worked loose and were in danger of falling off, while the stuffing boxes around her thrusting pistons were spewing out so much steam that Roberts feared his boilers would soon lose their pressure altogether. There was nothing for it but to heave to while the blades were secured and the stuffing boxes repacked. With the ship stopped and rolling in the troughs, this was difficult and dangerous work for the *Sirius*'s engineers. But the task was accomplished and the ship was soon under way again, undamaged by the seas and little delayed. During the brief stop, Roberts took the opportunity to check his bunkers. He was not encouraged to find that, with 1,700 miles yet to steam, only 250 tons of coal remained.

Some 550 miles astern, the *Great Western* was also in trouble. Hosken, who had been pushing his ship every bit as hard as his rival, was in the midst of a confrontation with his firemen. Exhausted by their labours in the stokehold and unable to rest when off watch because of the shock-like motion of the ship as she slammed into the seas, many of them were near breaking-point. Hosken had no sooner placated them than the larboard paddle-wheel began to shake so badly that it had to be stopped. Two bolts which were found to be missing were replaced and full speed was resumed. An hour or two later, a burst waterpipe in the engine-room caused a further delay. Hosken now began to despair of catching the *Sirius*, even though he had a superiority of at least two knots over the British & American ship.

17 April dawned like all the previous days for the *Sirius*. She was 350 miles to the south of Newfoundland and battling westwards against heavy seas and driving snow. To Roberts, as he haunted the tiny flying bridge for the thirteenth successive day, it seemed the nightmare would never end. Then, as the day

wore on, the snow began to thin and the wind fell away. By late afternoon the sombre canopy of cloud had drawn back, and as the sun went down, so did the sea. Just over a thousand miles ahead lay New York, and Roberts was at last able to contemplate victory. At that point his chief engineer informed him that barely 140 tons of coal were left in the bunkers.

Fast coming up astern but still burying her bows in green seas, the *Great Western* had fuel problems of her own, but not through any shortage. Hers was a problem of transportation. The coal remaining in her capacious bunkers, although ample to see the passage out, was all in the far ends of the ship and had to be wheeled in barrows to the stokehold amidships. It was a long haul, and her weary trimmers, who often found themselves pushing their barrows uphill as the ship climbed the waves, simply could no longer cope. The furnaces, starved of fuel, cooled and, as the steam pressure in the boilers fell back, the *Great Western* began to lose speed.

On the night of the 21st, the *Sirius* was to the south of the Nantucket Shoals, less than 200 miles from the Hudson river. The weather was fine and calm and she was surging ahead at eight knots. But all was not as well as it seemed, for her bunkers were almost empty of coal. Once the last precious lumps were gone and the dust was swept up, she would have to resort to her sails, and the magnificent efforts of all on board would have been in vain. She must either complete the voyage under steam or fail. Dick Roberts had an answer for this, too. Out came the axes and saws and into the hungry boiler furnaces went first the *Sirius*'s spare yards, then one of her masts and finally much of her expensive cabin furniture.

The *Sirius* limped into New York harbour on the night of 22 April, her tall funnel still belching smoke. Her momentous passage, made entirely under steam, had taken eighteen days and ten hours, and she had achieved an average speed of 6.7 knots. She was followed in some twelve hours later by the *Great Western*, only fifteen days out of Bristol. Hers was the fastest crossing to date of the North Atlantic, but she had lost the race.

The name of the *Great Western* still lives on, her likeness adorning the Blue Riband trophy fought over for so many years by the crack transatlantic liners that followed in her wake. As for the *Sirius*, having done all Junius Smith asked of her, in that she was the first ship ever to cross the Atlantic – or any other great ocean, for that matter – entirely under steam, she returned to the coastal trade and obscurity. Eight years later she came to an ignominious end on the rocks of Ballycotton Bay, and all that now recalls her triumph is the shabby figurehead in the Hull museum.

In 1938, one hundred years after the saga of the *Sirius* and *Great Western*, the 81,000-ton *Queen Mary* became the fastest merchant ship in the world by steaming from Cherbourg to New York in three days twenty-one hours forty-eight minutes at an average speed of 31.69 knots. She arrived in New York with all her cabin furniture intact.

4   The Point of Danger

In the mid-nineteenth century South Africa was in much the same state as it is now, with black fighting white for territory that historically belongs to neither. The Eighth Kaffir War, the latest in a seventy-year-long series of frontier skirmishes, was at its height. Hordes of Bantu tribesmen, pushed southwards by their old enemies the Zulus, were pouring across the frontiers of the Cape Colony into lands occupied by the British and their reluctant allies the Boers. British casualties were heavy, and towards the close of 1851 Sir Harry Smith, governor and commander-in-chief of the Cape, sent out a cry for help. This was to result in another of those peculiarly British blunders whose dreadful consequences are so often eclipsed by the sheer courage and fortitude of those involved.

London responded to Sir Harry's urgent call with uncharacteristic speed, and on 7 January 1852 Her Majesty's troop-ship *Birkenhead* sailed from Cork, bound for the Cape. On board were reinforcements consisting of 488 officers and men of no fewer than ten different regiments, including the 74th Foot (Royal Highland Fusiliers), the 91st Foot (Argyll & Sutherland Highlanders), the 6th Foot (Royal Warwickshire Regiment) and the 60th Rifles (Royal Greenjackets). In command of the troops for the voyage was Major Alexander Sefton of the 74th, a 37-year-old Scot from Aberdeenshire.

While the replacement officers and NCOs were regular and experienced members of the various regiments, the great majority of the troops were young Irish recruits, who had willingly 'taken the Queen's shilling' to escape from an Ireland still suffering from the Great Potato Famine of 1846. Most of these boys – and they were only mere boys of eighteen and nineteen – had never heard a shot fired in practice, let alone in battle. Few had seen the sea before, even fewer had set foot on a ship. To add to Major Sefton's temporary responsibilities, the troop-ship also carried twenty-five women and thirty-one children, wives and families of men serving in the Cape.

HMS *Birkenhead* was an iron-built paddle-steamer of 1,400 tons, 210 feet long and thirty-seven feet in the beam. She carried a crew of 129, including a detachment of six marines, and was commanded by Master-Commander Robert Salmond, a most experienced seaman and navigator whose naval ancestry went back to Elizabethan times. The *Birkenhead*'s builders claimed her to be a 'fast, comfortable, reliable and economical ship'. Captain Salmond and his crew would have it otherwise, and for good reasons. The ship had been built as a second-class frigate and shortly after completion had been found to be surplus to the fighting Navy's requirements and relegated to trooping. A forecastle and poop were added to her original flush deck, and troop decks were created below by cutting large openings in her watertight bulkheads, thereby effectively defeating the primary object of these bulkheads. When fully loaded with troops, coal and stores, the *Birkenhead* floated two feet below her original load waterline, giving her a freeboard of only five feet between her weather deck and the sea. In her new role she was slow, top-heavy and decidedly uncomfortable, if not unsafe.

It was blowing a full gale when the *Birkenhead* steamed out of Cork harbour on 7 January. She was to be dogged by foul weather for a full week until she was clear of the Bay of Biscay. With 673 souls crowded into such a small ship, conditions on board were appalling during those first days of the 6,000-mile voyage she had embarked on. Most of the recruits suffered the retching agonies of seasickness and were frightened to the point of panic by the violent movement of the ship. For the women the ordeal was even worse. Six were pregnant and went into premature labour brought on by the frenzied rolling and pitching, three died with their stillborn babies, and another of their number succumbed to tuberculosis. Three infants survived to add their untried lungs to the screams, groans and curses that filled the tween decks of the storm-tossed trooper.

When Biscay was at last astern, the weather moderated and some semblance of order was restored to the ship as she progressed southwards into a warmer and more equitable climate. Major Sefton, aware that morale amongst the troops was at a very low ebb, lost no time in bringing them up on deck for regular exercises and drill. The remainder of the voyage provided the young Irishmen with a thorough grounding in the discipline of the British Army, a discipline that was to be put to the test far sooner than anyone on board anticipated.

After brief calls at Madeira, Sierra Leone and St Helena for coal, water and provisions, the *Birkenhead* finally rounded the Cape of Good Hope on 23 February and dropped anchor off the naval base of Simonstown on that day. She had been six weeks and five days on passage.

Sir Harry Smith's needs must now have been even more acute, for, from the moment of arrival off Simonstown, the pressure was on Captain Salmond to sail again as quickly as possible. His orders were to take the troops to Algoa Bay and the Buffalo river, some 500 miles further up the coast. The ship was hurriedly refuelled and provisioned, horses were taken on for the officers of the regiments, and most of the woman and children were landed, leaving on board only seven women and thirteen children for the final stage of the voyage. When the *Birkenhead* was unceremoniously ushered out of Simonstown at six o'clock on the evening of the 25th, Captain Salmond and his crew had been working with little rest for almost forty-eight hours.

Fortunately the notoriously fickle Cape weather was on its best behaviour. But it was a black night, with the sea, undisturbed by even a cat's paw of wind, an undulating mirror, occasionally reflecting back the twinkling of the brighter stars. As she crossed the great expanse of False Bay, the measured thump of her engines loud in the silence of the night, the *Birkenhead* rolled easily in the long, lazy swell which came sweeping into the bay from the Southern Ocean.

Two hours after sailing, with the lights of Simonstown dipping astern, Captain Salmond and his sailing master, Mr Brodie, plotted the ship's position on the chart and set course for Cape Aghulas, ninety miles to the south-east. The two men waited until Cape Hangklip was cleared at 9.30, then, apparently satisfied that the ship would come to no harm, left the officer of the watch in charge and retired for the night. Having shouldered much of the burden of the hasty turn-around at Simonstown, both men were very tired. This may be why they failed to take account of certain unseen but crucial outside influences at work on the ship.

At midnight Mr J.O. Davies, second master, took over the

watch on the bridge. At the wheel was Able Seaman Thomas Coffin, while two lookouts were in the bow, and a leadsman, Able Seaman Abel Stone, was stationed on the port paddlebox sounding at regular intervals. The *Birkenhead* was making a steady 8½ knots on a course of south-south-east-½-east, with the low outline of the land just visible at three to four points on the port bow. All seemed well with the middle watch.

Shortly before two o'clock on the morning of the 26th, Abel Stone cast his lead and was surprised to find bottom at twelve fathoms. He immediately reported this to the officer of the watch, but Davies, either short on experience or long on fatigue, took no action to swing the ship away from the land, though she was obviously too close inshore. Ten minutes later the *Birkenhead* ran headlong onto an isolated pinnacle of rock just over a mile off the aptly named Danger Point.

Captain Salmond was on the bridge within two minutes of the ship's striking. Quickly assessing the situation, he ordered that a bower anchor be let go and the quarter-boats swung out and lowered to the water. His next action, which was to ring for full astern on the engines, proved to be a fatal mistake.

At first the *Birkenhead*'s churning paddle-wheels had no effect, then the ship began to draw slowly astern. The pinnacle of rock on which she was impaled sliced open her bottom like a can-opener at work on a sardine tin. A great rush of water swept into her lower troop decks, surging through the openings in her once-watertight bulkheads and flooding compartment after compartment. The fetid air rang with the pitiful cries of more than a hundred men as they were drowned in their hammocks.

On deck, in the ghostly light of the blue distress flares set off by the ship's gunner, John Archbold, the surviving troops, many of them half-naked, lunged wild-eyed in all directions. Women and children screamed, horses neighed and kicked, and all the while the stricken ship swung to and fro, grinding horribly on the rock that held her transfixed. It seemed that absolute panic was about to take hold, then Major Alexander Sefton drew his sword and stepped into the pages of the history books.

Calling on the troops to hold fast, Sefton, with the aid of his officers and NCOs, fell the men in on deck as though they were on a routine parade. Historians have long romanticized over this scene, portraying the troops in full uniform, drawn up in tight ranks and with fife and drum sounding defiance to the sea. In reality, the ranks were ragged, the men only partly clothed – some even naked – and all half-crazed with fear. Yet Sefton held them.

With order restored, Captain Salmond was able to begin the evacuation of the ship. First priority was given to the women and children, who were taken off in one of the quarter-boats already in the water. The second quarter-boat was then brought alongside, and one of the gigs successfully launched. Within a matter of minutes, the three boats were pulling away from the ship carrying eighty survivors. The boats were heavily laden, but the sea was still calm and they were in no danger.

At this point the operation began to go seriously wrong. It was found that the davit pins of the two paddlebox lifeboats were rusted in, and no amount of brawn could swing these boats out. The large boat the *Birkenhead* carried on deck amidships also proved useless, as there was no means of launching it. The second gig was swung out, but as it was being lowered, a tackle parted and the boat up-ended and was swamped. Of the seven lifeboats the troop-ship carried, only three had got away.

The catastrophe gathered pace. In the midst of the futile battle to launch the remaining boats, the *Birkenhead* broke her back. As she did so, her tall funnel crashed down, killing many of those still heaving on the tackles of the starboard paddlebox boat, including the sailing master, Mr Brodie. The whole fore part of the ship then broke off and sank, taking with it some sixty men who had been below manning the pumps in a hopeless bid to keep the sea at bay.

Those still alive retreated to the poop deck, the superb discipline of the troops continuing to hold. There was no more talk of lifeboats, for none remained. It would then have been easy for Sefton to give the word for every man to look to himself, but he feared that, in the ensuing fight to survive, the boat containing the women and children might be overwhelmed. And so they stood, shoulder to shoulder, more than 350 strong, awaiting the end. This came soon. With an anguished scream of rending metal, the after part of the *Birkenhead* split again and began to sink bodily. Only twenty minutes had passed since the ship first struck the rock which was forever after to bear her name.

Eight hours later the British schooner *Lioness*, passing Danger Point on her way to Capetown, sighted a boat inshore pulling towards her and signalling urgently. The *Lioness*, commanded by Captain Ramsden, stood in to investigate and soon learned of the awful tragedy of the night. She took thirty-seven survivors off the boat and then moved in towards the reported location of the wreck, on the way in coming upon the second lifeboat, which contained the *Birkenhead*'s women and children. Neither boat had been able to reach the shore, owing to the heavy surf.

When Ramsden arrived off the wreck during the afternoon, he found forty-three men clinging to the spars and rigging of the *Birkenhead*'s main topmast, all that remained of the trooper above water. After a fruitless search of the surrounding waters, the *Lioness* made all sail for Capetown, having on board 117 survivors in all.

Early next day Her Majesty's paddle-sloop *Radamanthus* arrived off Danger Point and sent in boats to pick up sixty-eight men who had made it to the shore on improvised rafts and scraps of wreckage. Of the others who stood fast on the poop when the *Birkenhead* went down – an estimated 290 troops and seamen, there was no sign. The scores of sharks that attended the sinking had done their work well.

When the final reckoning was made, it was found that only 184 of the *Birkenhead*'s total complement of 638 had survived. Captain Robert Salmond had gone, with sixty-seven of his crew, as had Major Alexander Sefton and 386 officers and men of the British Army.

There can be little argument as to the primary reason for the grounding of the *Birkenhead*. Captain Salmond, under pressure to make a fast passage to Algoa Bay, had set his course close inshore in order to avoid the full strength of the Agulhas Current, which flows north-westwards at up to two knots in this area. He also hoped to take advantage of counter-current setting in an east-south-easterly direction between Cape Hangklip and Cape Agulhas. Unfortunately he failed to make sufficient allowance for the inshore component of this current and for the effect of the swell, which throughout the night was relentlessly pushing the ship in towards the shore.

As to the subsequent sinking of the ship and the resultant terrible loss of life, much of the blame must lie with those who sanctioned the wilful destruction of the *Birkenhead*'s watertight integrity by the convenient piercing of her bulkheads. When first built, her hull had been divided into eight watertight compartments, and had this still been so when she struck the rock, the outcome of that dreadful night would have been very different.

Today the once lonely Birkenhead Rock is the scene of a great deal of unusual activity. The lure of a fortune in gold rumoured to have been in the *Birkenhead*'s strong-room when she went down has at last proved too much for the salvage men. The stern section of the wreck has been located and divers are probing the mud around it. In the low sandhills of Danger Point, where many of the *Birkenhead*'s heroes still sleep, there is an uneasy stirring.

5   The Long Haul

In the mid-1850s, with the Californian gold rush in full swing, hordes of fortune-hunters, drawn from all parts of the world, thronged the city of New York. Their aim was to secure the fastest possible transportation to the Pacific coast. The trans-America railway was still some twenty years away, and overland travel was often a dangerous gamble, sometimes ending in death by violence, starvation or thirst. The only route which offered these men a reasonable chance of survival lay on the sea, via Cape Horn. It was to this end that the first clipper ships were built. Their success was immediate.

The record time for the passage from New York to San Francisco was set up in 1851 by the Californian clipper *Flying Cloud*, built by the celebrated Donald Mackay of Boston. With every scrap of sail in her locker set, masts vibrating and sleek hull crashing through the water at speeds sometimes in excess of twenty knots, the *Flying Cloud* covered the 14,500 miles in question in eighty-nine days twenty-one hours.

In their day the clippers, and in particular those engaged in the China tea trade, were the subject of enormous publicity, sending the press into convulsions each time a sail was unfurled in earnest. Their evocative names were constantly on the lips of an admiring public on both sides of the Atlantic, and often in the four corners of the globe. The annual races from Foochow and Hong Kong to London were looked forward to with as much anticipation as the top sporting events of today. It was a poor man indeed who would not risk a wager, however small, on his favourite clipper ship.

Of course, it was easy for those safe on shore to endow the clippers with a romance all of their own. The clean lines and billowing white sails of these ships were enough to set the blood pumping in the stoniest of hearts. For the seamen involved, it was another matter. On the long voyages – and they were always long – the food was monotonous in the extreme and often too rotten for a starving man to eat. Such was the low freeboard of the clippers and so hard were they driven that the decks and accommodation were rarely dry, making life on and off watch a nightmare of dampness and discomfort. But all the hardships endured on deck paled into insignificance when a man went aloft. Here, on the swaying yardarms 150 feet above the sea, where the snapping canvas ran riot, it was an unending fight for survival – a fight which men lost with frightening regularity. Yet, despite all the hardships and dangers, there was immense prestige to be won, and few clipper men would have it otherwise.

The men who commanded the clippers were an elite, the likes of whom the world may never see again. Speed was their god, on whose altar they were prepared to sacrifice all human comfort, dignity and, when necessary, life itself. Obsessed with the need to pile on ever more and more sail, they would do so until it seemed the ship must drive herself under or, at the very least, lose her masts. But, with a foresight borne of long experience, they knew just how far to push their ship and the elements. Their mode of discipline was often so harsh as to be completely outside the law, even in those unenlightened days. They used fists, clubs and sometimes the gun to back up their orders. They were respected and cosseted by their owners, feared and hated by their crews but admired by all for their sheer, audacious professionalism.

The heyday of these 'wooden ships and iron men' was in the summer of 1866. In late May of that year, nine of Britain's finest clipper ships lay in the port of Foochow, on China's east coast, loading the first of the season's tea for the London market. The scene at the Pagoda Anchorage, eleven miles from the town and twenty-two from the sea, resembled a gathering of the clans, for eight of the tall ships were out of Scottish shipyards, and no fewer than five were wholly Scottish owned.

Once loaded, the clippers would match canvas and cunning in a 16,000-mile race across the oceans, whose object was to be the first ship into London Docks with the new season's tea. The successful captain would receive a personal bonus of £100, and his owners a premium of 10 shillings per ton on the cargo. In a day when many men counted their wealth in pennies, this was no mean inducement, but there was more at stake than mere gold. The men who sailed home the winning ship, from captain down to lowly cabin boy, would forever sit at the right hand of Poseidon, lord and master of the sea.

The race began on the evening of 29 May, when the *Ariel*, owned by Shaw, Lowther & Maxton of London, left Pagoda Anchorage in tow of the steam paddle-tug *Island Queen*. Commanded by Captain John Keay, a man noted for his iron discipline, the 853-ton, 197-foot long *Ariel* carried 25,451 square feet of canvas and had such fine lines that she was reputed to be able to glide through the water without a breath of wind to urge her on. Being the newest and largest of the clippers in the anchorage, she was the natural favourite with those placing money on the race in China and Britain. Loaded to her tropical marks with 14,000 chests of the finest teas, she looked set to cross the Min river bar at least twelve hours before her nearest challenger.

Activity in the anchorage increased to a fever pitch when the *Ariel* was seen pointing her long bowsprit downstream, for four other clippers were also very near to completion of loading. They were Scotland's best, the *Taeping*, 767 tons, owned by Alexander Rodger of Glasgow, the *Taitsing*, 815 tons, owned by Findlay & Longmuir of Greenock, the *Serica*, 708 tons, owned by James Findlay of Greenock, and the *Fiery Cross*, 689 tons, owned by John Campbell of Glasgow. The tension was high as the last of the tea-chests were manhandled into the hatch coamings of these ships. The *Fiery Cross* was the first to ship her hatchboards and tarpaulins, and so consumed with the need to get away was her master, Captain Richard Robinson, that he sailed without signing the bills of lading for his cargo.

Meanwhile, twenty miles downriver, the much-fancied *Ariel* had run out of luck. Her tug was not powerful enough to tow her across the bar, and she had been forced to anchor to await a slackening of the tide. Some hours later the *Fiery Cross*, in tow of a first-rate tug, glided past the anchored *Ariel* and headed out to sea. The night air rang loud with Captain Keay's bellows of frustration.

The *Ariel* finally reached the open sea fourteen hours later, in the forenoon of the 30th. By then the *Taeping*, commanded by Captain MacKinnon, and the *Serica*, Captain G. Innes, were snapping at her heels. The *Taitsing*, with Captain Daniel Knutsford in command, was the last of the vanguard to sail, crossing the Min river bar on the 31st.

The 16,000-mile race was now on in earnest, with the four Scots, *Fiery Cross*, *Serica*, *Taeping* and *Taitsing*, all determined to show their sterns to the lone English contender and favourite, the *Ariel*. The ships would follow a well-tried route down the South China Sea, passing first to the north and east of Formosa and then on a dog's-leg course across to the coast of Indochina and south to the Sunda Strait, gateway to the Indian Ocean. The South China Sea was, and still is, a most hazardous area, often cursed with poor visibility and dotted with low islands, sunken reefs and hidden shoals. In the nineteenth century it was poorly surveyed and accurate charts were hard to come by. The many wrecks on its reefs were stark memorials to those who had been foolish enough to ignore the old seafaring rule of 'lead, log and lookout'.

Running free before a fresh north-easterly wind, the *Fiery Cross* led the way through the Bashi Channel, which runs between Formosa and the Philippines, and by 3 June was passing to the north of the Paracels, an extensive group of low coral islands and reefs 180 miles to the east of what is now Vietnam. Holding his south-westerly course until within fifty miles of the coast, Robinson then brought the *Fiery Cross* around to head due south for the Natuna Islands, which lie to the north-west of Borneo and guard the approaches to the Sunda Strait. The wind was now in the south-west and freshening.

On 7 June, when to the east of Saigon, Robinson had the first sight of his pursuers since leaving the Min river, when a large, full-rigged ship appeared briefly on the horizon astern. This was the *Ariel*, with the formidable Captain Keay using all his considerable skills in an effort to overtake his Scottish rival. The other clippers, although out of sight, were close behind.

At the Sunda Strait, the narrow passage between Java and Sumatra, the ships were once again well strung out. *Fiery Cross* slipped past the doomed island of Krakatoa on the 18th, the *Ariel* and *Taeping* on the 20th and the *Serica*, with the *Taitsing* close in her wake, on the 22nd.

With strong south-easterly winds blowing in the Indian Ocean, all five ships made good time, the *Ariel* on one occasion logging 330 miles in a day and the *Fiery Cross* 328. The Scottish ship crossed to the south of Mauritius on 30 June, with the *Ariel* still lagging two days behind. At the Cape of Good Hope, which the *Fiery Cross* rounded on 15 July, the *Ariel* had gained a day and was pushing hard. Their nearest challenger, the *Serica*, was six days astern.

Once in the South Atlantic, despite the favourable run of the Benguela Current and strong south-east trades, the race lost its momentum. The *Fiery Cross* did not reach the Equator until sunset on 4 August, having averaged only 160 miles a day from the Cape. A few days later she hit the Doldrums and came to an abrupt halt. On the 9th, while Robinson still fumed and trimmed his sails to tempt every passing cat's paw of wind, MacKinnon's *Taeping* clawed her way over the southern horizon. Sailing fitfully, the two ships kept company for the next eight days. During this time there was no sight or sound of the others. Robinson and MacKinnon now assumed that the outcome of the race would be decided between them. They were to be proved wrong.

By 17 August the *Fiery Cross* and the *Taeping* had reached the furthest point west in their long, curving sweep out into the Atlantic. They were a thousand miles west of the Canaries and sniffing at the southern edge of the north-east trades when the *Taeping* caught a favourable wind and, lifting her skirts, disappeared over the horizon. With the *Fiery Cross* still becalmed, it was Robinson's turn to taste bitter disappointment.

A further dramatic change of fortune occurred at the Azores. For the first time since her ill-fated attempt to be first across the Min river bar some three months earlier, the London-registered *Ariel* went into the lead. The *Taeping*, *Fiery Cross* and *Serica* were in hot pursuit, all four ships passing Flores on the same day. The *Taitsing* was three days behind and fighting to make up lost ground. With 1,500 miles to go and all ships running free before the prevailing south-westerly winds, it was still anyone's race, but the *Ariel*, with her greater sail area, had a slight advantage. Much would now depend on the individual sailing skills of the clipper masters.

As dawn broke off the Lizard on 5 September, the *Ariel* was alone and confidently in the lead when, to Captain Keay's amazement and chagrin, the *Taeping* loomed up out of the haze astern. MacKinnon, on the *Taeping*, was no less surprised, for the two ships had not seen each other for more than seventy days. Keay and MacKinnon were old rivals, both having at one time commanded the legendary *Ellen Rodger*, one of the fastest clippers ever to grace the China trade. The two men now prepared to do battle on a personal basis, the England/Scotland factor taking second place.

Crowding on every available stitch of canvas, the *Ariel* and *Taeping* raced up the Channel side by side, running their gunwales under before a stiff west-south-westerly. At daybreak on the 6th they picked up their pilots off Dungeness within minutes of each other and thundered on up through the Straits of Dover to the Downs. Here they were taken in tow by tugs and continued into the Thames Estuary. Unknown to them, the *Serica* was a bare four hours astern.

Once more, as at Foochow, the balance of this great sailing race was tipped by steam. The *Taeping* had secured the best tug, and she docked in London at 9.45 that night, just short of ninety-nine days on passage. Captain Keay, his blood pressure at boiling-point, brought the *Ariel* to her berth half an hour later, while the *Serica* locked in at 11.30 on the last of the tide. The unfortunate *Fiery Cross* did not reach the Downs until the 7th and was there forced to anchor to ride out a gale. She berthed at eight o'clock on the morning of the 8th. The back-marker in the race, the *Taitsing*, arrived in the river on the 11th.

Officially, the Scottish *Taeping* took the honours by a bowsprit, but there were no real winners in the race of 1866. With so many clippers arriving in the port within the space of a few days, the London market found itself with several million pounds of new tea on its hands – half a year's consumption for the whole of Britain, in fact. Prices fell heavily, and from then on it was decided to discontinue the cargo premium for the first ship home. The annual clipper races still went on, but they were never the same again.

The gruelling clipper trade was the ultimate test of man and ship, the perfect marriage of human tenacity and skill with the products of the world's finest shipyards. But the sacrifices called for and the risks taken inevitably exacted a heavy toll. Men grew old before their time, died before their time; ships were lost when they should not have been lost. Captain MacKinnon, of the victorious *Taeping*, died in Capetown on his next voyage, worn out at forty-one. Five years later the *Taeping* was lost when she ran onto Ladd's Reef in the South China Sea, while on a voyage from Amoy to New York. Captain Innes died in the *Serica*, with all but one of his crew, when she was wrecked on the

Paracels in 1872. In that same year the gallant *Ariel* also met her end, pooped while running her easting down in the Roaring Forties. Only the *Taitsing* and the *Fiery Cross* lived on into old age. The *Taitsing* was lost off the coast of Zanzibar in 1883, and the once-proud *Fiery Cross* came to a sad end in 1889, when she sank in the River Medway with her cargo of coal on fire. So the mighty fell, but they will never be forgotten.

6 The Scapegoat

After lying undisturbed in her grave 13,000 feet deep in the North Atlantic for seventy-seven years, the *Titanic* has already felt the searching eye of the underwater camera and the scrape of the salvage man's probe. Speculation has it that she may one day suffer the final affront of exhumation.

There is treasure, so it is said, which would now be worth up to £80 million, in the sunken liner's safe, but more likely this is just a product of the imagination of certain journalists of her day. If successful, however, such a major feat of salvage would arouse intense excitement around the world, thus proving extremely lucrative for the participants, but it would be unlikely to answer many of the questions posed by the loss of the great ship. It would certainly do nothing to clear the name of the saddest victim of the *Titanic*'s sinking, Captain Stanley Lord, master of the British steamer *Californian*. Lord, it was alleged, stood by and watched more than 1,500 people die without lifting a finger to help. In reality, Captain Lord was nothing more than a convenient scapegoat who was used to divert attention from the shame of the world's first 'unsinkable' liner, which went down so tragically on its maiden voyage.

The *Titanic*, at 46,382 tons and 853 feet long, was in 1912 the largest ship ever built; she was also the most luxurious liner afloat. Owned by the Oceanic Steam Navigation Company, popularly known as 'the White Star Line', she had a service speed of twenty-two knots and was certified by the Board of Trade to carry 3,547 passengers and crew. She was equipped with the new wireless telegraphy, and her lifeboats were fitted with the latest Welin mechanical davit system, which was said to ensure fast and trouble-free launching of the boats in the event of an emergency. Not that any situation involving the abandonment of this grand vessel was ever envisaged. Her cellular double bottom – another brilliant innovation – and fourteen watertight compartments made her unsinkable in the eyes of all associated with her. The *Titanic* was her own lifeboat.

The *Titanic* left Southampton on her maiden voyage at noon on 10 April 1912, bound for New York. She made brief stops at Cherbourg and Queenstown, embarking at the latter port a contingent of Irish emigrants. When she sailed from Queenstown on the afternoon of the 11th, she had on board a total complement of 2,201, made up of 885 crew and 1,316 passengers, less than half the number she was equipped to carry. Her first-class passenger list included a number of millionaires, diplomats and famous names in industry and commerce, among whom were John Jacob Astor, Sir Cosmo Duff Gordon, Baron von Drachstedt, Charles Melville Hayes, president of the Grand Trunk Railway, and J.P. Thayer, president of the Pennsylvania Railroad. They were all in good hands, for in command of the *Titanic* was 59-year-old Captain Edward Smith, a master mariner of great experience, on his last voyage before retirement. Smith's senior navigating officers, Chief Officer H.F. Wilde and First Officer Murdoch, both held extra master's certificates and were also very experienced men. This being a maiden voyage, at Captain Smith's shoulder – and possibly peering over it all too often – were J. Bruce Ismay, chairman of the White Star Line, and Thomas Andrew, managing director of the ship's builders, Harland & Wolff of Belfast. The weather in the North Atlantic was unusually fair, and it was hoped to complete the 3,100-mile crossing in just under six days, the liner being scheduled to reach New York on the 16th.

Having cleared Fastnet Rock at about 17.00 on the 11th, the *Titanic*'s engines were worked up to full speed, and a course was set for New York which would take the liner to the south of the iceberg zone.

If, in the North Atlantic, the uninterrupted raging of the wind and sea is the greatest danger facing the mariner in winter, in spring and early summer it is the iceberg. Calved from the glaciers of Greenland, the Atlantic icebergs drift southwards, borne on the cold Labrador Current, which increases in velocity as the sun moves north from the Equator. During their long journey south these bergs, which may be up to 450 feet high and 1,500 feet long at the time of their birth, lose much of their bulk as they move into a warmer climate. The smaller bergs melt away altogether, but the larger ones, floating with nine-tenths of their mass below the surface, end up on the southern edge of the Grand Banks of Newfoundland. Keeping close company with these icebergs are fields of pack-ice, often swarming with young seals, which were once much sought-after by the sealing fleets of the world.

For transatlantic ships bound for New York, April is the month of greatest peril, as this is when the ice reaches furthest south before finding extinction in the warm waters of the Gulf Stream. In this respect, April of 1912 was a particularly bad month, with no fewer than 395 large icebergs recorded as having crossed to the south of latitude 48°N. Had Captain Smith been privy to this knowledge at the time, the course of history might have been changed.

By noon on the 14th, the *Titanic* was just under halfway across the Atlantic and behind schedule. At twenty-two knots, as she had been averaging, she would not reach her berth in New York until well after dark on the 16th. From the White Star Line's point of view, this was most undesirable. A great deal of publicity had been laid on for the vessel's arrival, much of which would be wasted unless she steamed up the Hudson river in daylight. After conferring with Bruce Ismay and Thomas Andrew, Captain Smith instructed his chief engineer to increase speed. It was imperative that the *Titanic* arrive on her berth not later than 17.00 on the 16th.

During the afternoon, the liner's wireless-operator John Phillips began to receive a stream of radio messages from other ships warning of the presence of icebergs. It soon became clear that an extensive icefield located between latitudes 41°25′N and and 42°00′N was drifting south into the *Titanic*'s path. The danger was sufficient to warrant an alteration of course to the south in order to avoid the bergs, but as this would add more miles to the passage, Captain Smith declined to do so. There is no evidence that Ismay brought any pressure to bear on him, but Smith was certainly determined to keep a daylight appointment with New York's newspapermen.

When darkness fell on the 14th, the *Titanic* was to the south of the Grand Banks of Newfoundland and steaming at 22½ knots under a clear, starlit sky. There was no moon, but the visibility was exceptional and the sea a flat, oily calm rarely seen in those latitudes. However, the air was bitterly cold, and most passengers remained below decks, whiling away the evening in the ship's sumptuously appointed saloons or, in the case of the emigrants, huddled close in the steerage for warmth. All classes were agreed that the rock-like steadiness of the liner inspired confidence in even the poorest sailors amongst them.

High above the accommodation, on the *Titanic's* bridge, the atmosphere was one of low-key vigilance as she sliced her way through the black water on that tranquil April night. Extra lookouts had been posted and the officers on watch spent a great deal of time scanning the horizon ahead through their night glasses. If there were icebergs about, it was assumed they would be seen in good time to alter course.

In the wireless office John Phillips had other things on his mind. With New York only two days away, the liner's millionaire passengers were again taking up the reins of their various business enterprises, and Phillips and his junior, Harold Bride, were inundated with messages to send to the shore station at Cape Race, Newfoundland. At 19.30, during a lull in transmissions, Phillips listened in to a warning broadcast by the 6,233-ton Leyland Line ship *Californian* reporting three large icebergs in sight five miles to the south of her. The position given was fifty miles ahead of the *Titanic* and directly in her path. Phillips apparently did not realize the significance of the warning and consequently delayed passing the message to the bridge for some time. Meanwhile the *Titanic* ploughed on through the night at maximum speed.

Soon after 21.30 Phillips heard the steamer *Mesaba* reporting the sighting of very heavy pack ice and numerous large bergs. Again the position given lay on the track being followed by the *Titanic*. At that moment, another clutch of messages to be sent arrived in the wireless office, and the *Mesaba's* warning was put on file, to be delivered to the bridge when convenient.

The night moved on, and the messages to be sent piled up on Phillips' desk. He was now experiencing difficulty in raising Cape Race, and when, at 23.00. the *Californian's* operator, Cyril Evans, broke into his transmissions to report his ship stopped and surrounded by ice, a harassed Phillips told him to get off the air. Mildly annoyed at this rebuff, Evans, the *Californian's* only operator, threw down his headphones and went off watch for the night.

At twenty minutes before midnight on 14 April, the lookout in the *Titanic*'s crow's nest, Able Seaman Frederick Fleet, became aware of a darker shadow on the horizon dead ahead of the ship. As he strained his eyes to pierce the blackness, the shadow grew larger and gained in substance at a frightening speed. With a sharp intake of breath, Fleet lunged for the bridge telephone.

The urgent report from the crow's nest of an iceberg ahead seems to have been received on the liner's bridge with some scepticism, for many more precious seconds ticked by before avoiding-action was taken. At last, under the influence of full helm, the *Titanic*'s bows swung slowly to port, and a towering island of glistening ice slid down her starboard side. To those on the bridge, it seemed that disaster had been narrowly averted, then the great liner rolled gently to port as she ripped open her bottom on the underwater shelf of the iceberg. The senior officer on the bridge, First Officer Murdoch, rang the engines to stop and then full astern before throwing the switch to close all watertight doors. The *Titanic* came to rest half a mile beyond the berg, which by then had been swallowed up by the darkness again.

Below decks, the impression was that the ship had been jostled by an unseen hand and, although some eyebrows were raised, few had any idea that a catastrophe had befallen them. Not until Captain Smith and his senior officers had made a hurried tour of the bowels of the ship was it realized that there was a gash of 300 feet long in the liner's bottom. Five of her watertight compartments were already flooded. The pumps were set going, but they were unable to deal with the ingress of water. The designers of this 'unsinkable' ship had omitted to carry her watertight bulkheads above D Deck, and as her bows sank lower, the sea spilled over into the next compartment aft, progressively flooding the hull as she settled in the water. The mighty *Titanic* was doomed.

Shortly after midnight, with the ship still deceptively upright but with the sea pouring into her ruptured hull at an unstoppable rate, Smith ordered the lifeboats cleared away. Moments later he passed the word for all passengers to don lifejackets and report to their boat stations. This order failed to cause more than a general stir of annoyance, for the majority of passengers refused to believe that a serious emergency had arisen. To them, the thought of leaving the warmth of the accommodation to line up on deck like sheep on such a cold night seemed pointless, if not idiotic. Many went back to bed.

On the bridge, the full horror of the situation was all too apparent. Not only was the ship clearly sinking but, in view of her inadequate lifeboat capacity – a shortcoming not revealed to the passengers, it was certain that, unless help came quickly, more than half her complement would have to go down with her.

In 1912 there were few rules governing life-saving equipment in ships, and the number of lifeboats carried was left to the discretion of the owners. Although the *Titanic* was certified for a maximum complement of 3,547, she had only eighteen lifeboats, with a total capacity of a thousand persons. White Star was obviously of the opinion that only a token number of lifeboats was necessary for their new liner, these serving merely to inspire confidence in the faint-hearted, should there be any.

At 00.15 on the 15th, Captain Smith ordered John Phillips to send out a distress. This was picked up by a number of ships, but all were many hours' steaming away. It was only by pure chance that at 00.30 Harold Cottam, wireless-operator of the Cunard liner *Carpathia*, bound from New York to Gibraltar, decided to call the *Titanic* before he retired to his bunk. Cottam was astonished when his perfunctory call was immediately answered with an urgent burst of morse. Phillips rapped out, 'SOS SOS. COME AT ONCE. WE HAVE STRUCK BERG. POSITION 41°46'N 50°14'W. SOS'. This was the first time the new distress signal 'SOS' had been used at sea.

The 13,603-ton *Carpathia*, commanded by Captain Arthur Rostron, was at this time fifty-eight miles south-east of the *Titanic*. Knowing the fearful risk he was running – the *Carpathia* had on board 735 passengers and 300 crew, Rostron turned his ship about and raced north-west at sixteen knots through the ice-strewn area, praying that he would arrive in time.

Aboard the *Titanic*, Smith had given the order to swing out the boats, and her officers were attempting to embark the women and children, numbering 544 in all. The men, those who might be lucky enough to find a place in the boats, would have to wait their turn. Hopes were suddenly raised when, just before 01.00 on the 15th, the lights of another ship were seen close by – between eight and ten miles off, those on the bridge of the *Titanic* estimated. Distress rockets were sent up and flares lit but, although at one time the other ship seemed to be moving towards the liner, she did not answer her signals and suddenly altered course and made off into the night.

And so the great drama being played out in mid-Atlantic drew inexorably to its close. In the early hours of the morning of 15 April, Captain Edward Smith found himself in command of a sinking ship, with sufficient boats to take off fewer than half those on board. This iniquity was compounded by the reluctance of passengers to leave a ship they had been assured was unsinkable, and the inability of many of the emigrants to find their way up on deck from the bowels of the ship where they were berthed. In the ensuing confusion, a number of boats went away only part-loaded; at least one sixty-man boat carried only twelve people, seven of whom were crew members. In all, only 336 women, 52 children and 315 men escaped the sinking ship in lifeboats. With the sea temperature at a lethal 28°F, those unfortunate enough to end up in the water would not survive for many minutes.

At 02.05 John Phillips sent his last message: 'COME AS QUICKLY AS POSSIBLE. ENGINE-ROOM FILLING UP TO BOILERS.' Fifteen minutes later, the 46,382-ton *Titanic* heaved her stern high in the air and slid bow-first to her last resting-place beneath the waves. When the *Carpathia* arrived on the scene at 04.00, she found the sea littered with wreckage, amongst which floated the bodies of those who had stayed with the ship. From the lifeboats, found rowing in aimless circles, she took on board 703 souls, the only survivors out of the liner's total complement of 2,201.

It cannot be disputed that the unshakeable belief of the *Titanic*'s builders, owners and captain in the liner's complete invulnerability was the primary cause of her loss. Over the intervening years, the myth of the 'unsinkable' ship has been well and truly exploded, but in 1912, when shipbuilding was in the throes of a new and exciting revolution, there seemed to be no end to man's growing ascendancy over the sea. The *Titanic*, with her double-skinned bottom and fourteen watertight compartments, each capable of being isolated at the touch of a switch, was genuinely thought to be unsinkable. There can be no other explanation for Captain Smith's decision to press on through that black night at 22½ knots when he had already received ample warning of icebergs in his path. It has been suggested, but never proved, that Smith – perhaps urged on by the line's chairman and the ship's builder – was attempting to make a record crossing on this maiden voyage. The weather throughout the passage had been the best seen in the North Atlantic for many years, and the temptation to go for a record must have been very strong. It is certain, however, that Smith was under pressure to make every attempt to berth in New York before dark on the 16th.

Tragically, while the *Titanic* was foundering, the *Californian*, commanded by 34-year-old Captain Stanley Lord, lay stopped just out of sight over the horizon. Owing to the presence of heavy ice, Captain Lord had stopped his ship at the onset of darkness on the 14th and was drifting, awaiting daylight before proceeding. Her wireless-operator, Cyril Evans, who had tried unsuccessfully to warn the *Titanic* of the danger she faced, was sleeping soundly in his bunk. A little before 01.00 on the 15th, the *California*'s officer of the watch saw rockets bursting low down on the horizon. He called Captain Lord, who by then had also turned in for the night. It seems Lord accepted the report without concern and took no action.

At the two subsequent courts of inquiry into the disaster, it was argued, and accepted, that the *Californian* must have been the ship seen by the *Titanic*'s officers before they fired their distress rockets. On the evidence of the same officers, it was also accepted that the *Californian* was only eight to ten miles off and must therefore have witnessed in full the sinking of the liner. Even though he produced his ship's log-book, which gave the *Californian*'s position as nineteen miles off the *Titanic*, and consequently below the visible horizon, Lord was already damned in the eyes of the world. As to the rockets seen by his officer of the watch, Lord said he had believed these to be signals between ships of the same line or between fishing vessels in the area, both practices being common at the time. At the court of inquiry, Lord was called only as a witness, and no charges were laid against him, but it was made quite clear that the courts believed he had callously left more than 1,500 people to die on that night, and he was therefore the villain of the sad affair. The world's press took up the theme with relish, and all the frustration and outrage generated by the loss of the 'unsinkable' ship were directed at a man who had not been given the chance to defend himself. The whitewash of the White Star fiasco was complete.

For many years, with the help of his professional association, Captain Stanley Lord fought to clear his name, but without success. The stigma of the *Titanic* stayed with him until the day of his death, in January 1961. Ironically, shortly after he died, evidence emerged which, had it been produced at the courts of inquiry, would most certainly have exonerated him. This was a statement made in 1912 by Henrik Naess, first mate of the Norwegian sealer *Samson*, to the Norwegian consul in Iceland. Naess testified that on the night of 14/15 April 1912 the *Samson* had been illegally taking seals from the ice floes on the southern edge of the Grand Banks of Newfoundland. At some time after midnight, Naess and others saw rockets, flares and bright lights close by. It was assumed that the pyrotechnics were signals between US naval vessels searching for seal-poachers, and the *Samson*'s master, not wishing to be caught, recalled his boats and made off at speed. As the sealer had no radio, it was not until she reached Iceland that her crew heard of the loss of the *Titanic*. The *Samson*'s master was, understandably, reluctant to make public his clandestine activities off the Grand Banks, but Henrik Naess, appalled by the magnitude of the disaster, felt compelled to speak out.

It has never been satisfactorily explained why the testimony of Henrik Naess lay undisclosed for fifty years but, in view of this evidence, it seems almost certain that the ship seen from the bridge of the *Titanic* was the *Samson* and not the *Californian*. Captain Stanley Lord may now rest easy in his grave; the same cannot be said for the *Titanic*.

Fortunately tragedies of the scale of the sinking of the *Titanic* invariably close stable doors which have been left open. In this case, an International Ice Patrol was set up, and new rules were introduced regarding life-saving appliances on all ships. The modern cruise liner is obliged to carry sufficient lifeboats and inflatable rafts to evacuate her total complement more than twice over.

7 The Curse of
Fryatt's Gold Watch

On the morning of 17 February 1917 the German submarine *U-33* was fifty-five miles west of the Fastnet Rock and idling at periscope depth awaiting a suitable victim. When he sighted an old British collier trailing black smoke across the horizon, the commander of *U-33* gave a grunt of satisfaction and laid his sights carefully. The torpedo struck the collier just abaft her engine-room and exploded with a loud roar, sending a column of water and debris high in the air. Seen through the periscope, the scene aboard the doomed merchant ship followed a familiar pattern, her crew swarming like panic-stricken ants as they struggled to lower the boats before their ship sank under them.

Although the collier was noticeably lower in the water, she did not sink at once, and the impatient German commander brought the U-boat to the surface to administer the *coup de grâce* by shellfire. The water was still streaming off her casings as her gun's crew raced forward to man the gun, but they were too late. Their innocent-looking victim opened her side ports, dropped her dummy deck-houses and opened fire with five 12-pounders, two 6-pounders and a Maxim gun. His Majesty's Ship *Q5*, commanded by Lieutenant-Commander Gordon Campbell, sent *U-33* spiralling to the bottom, leaving only two men in the water to be rescued. The curse of Fryatt's gold watch had been lifted.

Charles Fryatt, born in December 1872, went to sea in the North Sea ferries of the Great Eastern Railway Company as a young ordinary seaman. By the time he was forty, he had risen through the ranks to command the 1,380-ton *Brussels*, which plied regularly between Harwich and the Hook of Holland with passengers and freight. Built at Dundee in 1901, the *Brussels* was regarded as one of the best of her day. Fryatt, who was a dedicated, first-rate seaman, was proud to command her. The men who served under him did so with equal pride.

The outbreak of war in 1914 had little effect on the Great Eastern ferries, which continued to keep open the link between Britain and the neutral Netherlands, much as they had in times of peace. German U-boats were operating in the North Sea but, under the international 'Cruiser Rules', they were constrained from sinking any merchant ship before she had been stopped, her papers examined and her crew allowed to take to the boats. Whether it suited the Germans to allow the Harwich – Hook route to continue or whether the ferries were just too fast for the U-boats has never been made clear. Certainly for many months after the outbreak of hostilities they left the Great Eastern ships well alone.

The situation took a dramatic turn for the worse when, in February 1915, Berlin issued a decree to the effect that all merchant ships found in British waters would be sunk on sight, regardless of their cargo. A few days later Captain Fryatt received top secret orders from the Admiralty instructing him how best to act when threatened by a U-boat. The *Brussels*, like all British merchantmen at the time, was unarmed, and Their Lordships advised that, when challenged, her best course of action would be to steam straight at the U-boat, forcing her to dive. The order was, if not suicidal, certainly imprudent, for few merchant ships have bows strong enough to withstand ramming a submarine. However, Fryatt, with a twin-screw, fifteen-knot ship under his command, doubted he would ever find it necessary to take such drastic action. He was proved right when, on 3 March, the *Brussels* was threatened by a surfaced U-boat and he was able to avoid trouble simply by running away at top speed.

But escape was not always to be so easy. Three weeks later, on the afternoon of 28 March, when the *Brussels* was off the Maas lightship and nearing the end of her regular crossing from Harwich, she ran into an ambush. Fryatt, who was on the bridge with Chief Officer Hartnell, was first to spot the submarine, on the surface and closing purposefully on the ferry's starboard bow. *U-33*, one of Germany's latest and most powerful submarines, commanded by Korvetten-Kapitän Gausser, was moving in to challenge.

Gausser signalled the *Brussels* to stop, but Fryatt, being only a few miles from Dutch territorial waters, had no intention of surrendering his ship. Calmly he called for maximum engine revolutions and altered course to starboard to pass astern of the submarine. Gausser countered by bringing *U-33* sharply round to port, so that her bows pointed directly at the exposed port side of the British ship.

Fearful that the U-boat was manoeuvring to torpedo his ship, Fryatt decided that the time had come to put the Admiralty's plan to the test. Instructing Hartnell to warn the engine-room, Fryatt altered course to port and put the submarine right ahead. The *Brussels* was by now making a good seventeen knots, and for a while it was touch and go for *U-33*. She only narrowly avoided being run down by executing an undignified crash dive. When an angry Gausser brought her back to the surface, his intended victim was inside Dutch waters and out of his grasp.

The German Navy, humiliated by this apparently contemptuous treatment of one of their best submarines by an unarmed British merchant ship, was furious. Fryatt, who maintained he had not really intended to ram the U-boat, was branded as a pirate and a potential murderer. How Charles Fryatt, a peaceable, God-fearing master mariner going about his lawful business, could be regarded as a pirate is beyond conception. His action in taking a run at the U-boat may have been prompted by the Admiralty's instruction, but it was also the instinctive action of a man intent on saving his own ship.

Their Lordships, on the other hand, were elated at this successful implementation of their policy and gave it maximum publicity. Fryatt and his officers received national acclaim, their defiance of the enemy was praised in the House of Commons, and Fryatt, his chief officer and chief engineer were presented with suitably inscribed gold watches by a grateful nation.

Charles Fryatt, fiercely proud of his gold hunter, carried it with him at all times. Friends and colleagues urged him to be careful, arguing that, if he were captured, the watch might prove provocative to the Germans. Fryatt would have none of this. Where he went, his watch went. It had become a talisman to him. His senior officers, on the other hand, preferred to leave their watches at home while they were at sea.

Meanwhile, all three continued to play their part in keeping open the tenuous link between Britain and the Netherlands. Unknown to them, the German naval authorities were quietly fuming at their disgrace, and the word had gone out that the *Brussels* must be brought to book, whatever the cost. Over the next twelve months, numerous attempts were made to sink or capture the ferry, but each time her speed and Fryatt's skilful seamanship enabled her to escape.

Late on the night of 22 June 1916, the *Brussels* sailed from the Hook of Holland, bound for Harwich with the usual passengers and cargo. As she was pulling away from the quay, those on her bridge were surprised to see a signal rocket curving skywards from the beach beyond the Hook. This was an unusual sight in wartime, even in these neutral waters, but Fryatt gave it only a moment's thought before he turned his attention to conning the ship down river.

The Maas lightship, its powerful beam sweeping the wavetops four times in every twenty seconds, was passed just before midnight, and the *Brussels* steamed out into the North Sea on a west-south-westerly course. It was a black night and, as was customary, the ferry was showing all her lights. An hour later Fryatt, who might easily have taken the opportunity to go below, was still on the bridge with Chief Officer Hartnell. There was an uneasy tension on the bridge; even the dark outline of a fishing-boat drifting past without lights had a sinister look to it. When the fisherman was abeam, a shaded signal lamp could be seen flashing seawards from her bridge, and Fryatt's suspicions came to a head. Coincidence could not explain both the flaring rocket on sailing from the Hook and this idling drifter signalling their passing. He called to Hartnell to extinguish all lights and send the passengers below decks.

The *Brussels* continued on her course at full speed, with Fryatt and Hartnell sweeping the horizon ahead and to port and starboard with their night glasses. Soon another darkened ship was seen approaching on a collision course, and Fryatt was forced to switch on his navigation lights to warn her off. This was a move he lived to regret. Fifteen minutes later the *Brussels* was surrounded by a flotilla of German destroyers, all with their guns manned and threatening to open fire if she did not heave to. This time their could be no running away and, mindful of the safety of his passengers, Fryatt had no alternative but to stop his ship.

At daybreak on 23 June the *Brussels*, with the German ensign at her stern, was escorted into Zeebrugge and then piloted up the canal to Bruges, some seven miles inland. Here she was secured, and her passengers and crew were taken ashore under guard. The passengers, many of them neutrals, were soon released for repatriation, but Fryatt and his crew were marched to the local gaol. Next day, with the exception of Fryatt and Hartnell, the crew of the *Brussels*, which included six stewardesses, were sent to Germany for internment.

Fryatt, who had accepted the taking of his ship calmly, was not unduly disturbed when he was separated from Hartnell and put into solitary confinement. Again, when the long interrogation began and his treasured gold watch with its incriminating inscription was produced, he showed little surprise. He had guessed what the Germans were about. They were determined to make an example of him in return for the humiliation of *U-33*, and the watch was there to prove the case. Undeterred, he stuck to his story that he had merely taken a run at the U-boat to force her to dive, not to ram and sink her, as his interrogators would have it. Fryatt considered that, under international law, the very worst his captors could do would be to throw him into a prison camp for the rest of the war. But he underestimated the fury of the Germans.

On 28 July Reuters in Amsterdam received the following official telegram from Berlin:

ON JULY 27, AT BRUGES, BEFORE THE COURT MARTIAL OF THE MARINE CORPS, THE TRIAL TOOK PLACE OF CAPT. CHARLES FRYATT OF THE BRITISH STEAMER 'BRUSSELS', WHICH WAS BROUGHT IN AS A PRIZE. THE ACCUSED WAS CONDEMNED TO DEATH BECAUSE, ALTHOUGH HE WAS NOT A MEMBER OF A COMBATANT FORCE, HE MADE AN ATTEMPT ON THE AFTERNOON OF THE 28TH MARCH 1915 TO RAM THE GERMAN SUBMARINE U-33 NEAR THE MAAS LIGHTSHIP. THE ACCUSED, AS WELL AS THE FIRST OFFICER AND CHIEF ENGINEER OF THE STEAMER, RECEIVED AT THE TIME FROM THE BRITISH ADMIRALTY A GOLD WATCH AS A REWARD FOR HIS BRAVE CONDUCT ON THAT OCCASION, AND HIS ACTION WAS MENTIONED WITH PRAISE IN THE HOUSE OF COMMONS. ON THE OCCASION IN QUESTION, DISREGARDING THE U-BOAT'S SIGNAL TO STOP AND SHOW HIS NATIONAL FLAG, HE TURNED AT THE CRITICAL MOMENT AT HIGH SPEED ON THE SUBMARINE, WHICH ESCAPED THE STEAMER

BY A FEW METRES ONLY BY IMMEDIATELY DIVING. HE CONFESSED
THAT IN DOING SO HE ACTED IN ACCORDANCE WITH THE
INSTRUCTIONS OF THE ADMIRALTY. THE SENTENCE WAS CON-
FIRMED YESTERDAY AFTERNOON AND CARRIED OUT BY SHOOTING.
ONE OF THE MANY NEFARIOUS 'FRANC TIREUR' PROCEEDINGS OF
THE BRITISH MERCHANT MARINE AGAINST OUR WAR VESSELS HAS
THUS FOUND A BELATED BUT MERITED EXPIATION.

The news that Charles Fryatt had been taken out onto a piece
of waste ground in the Bruges dockland and shot shocked the
civilized world. Not since the execution of Nurse Edith Cavell in
October 1915 had the international telegraph wires hummed so
loud. Charles Fryatt did not therefore die in vain. His death
evoked a great surge of world opinion against Germany, which
was eventually to contribute to her defeat.

After the war, Fryatt's body was exhumed and brought back to
Britain, to be laid to rest at Dovercourt, where he had lived with
his wife and children, and overlooking the port of Harwich
which had been journey's end to him for so many years. Today
Charles Fryatt is forgotten, his name living on only in an
obscure fund set up in his memory by the Imperial Service
Guild to bring succour to mariners incarcerated in foreign gaols.
It is not recorded what happened to the gold watch that sealed
his fate.

Fryatt's ship, the *Brussels*, on the other hand, lived on into a
somewhat undignified old age. For the remainder of the war she
was used as a depot ship at Zeebrugge, ironically serving
German submarines based at the port. When the end of the war
was in sight, the Germans scuttled her before they retreated
from Zeebrugge. It was August 1919 before she was raised by a
British salvage team. Two years later, having been extensively
repaired, she was sold to J. Gale & Company of Preston and
spent the next 7½ years running cattle between Dublin and
Preston. When fully loaded, she was able to carry 600 cattle and
a thousand sheep, a far cry from her proud days on the Harwich
– Hook run. In April 1929, old, rusting and permeated with the
smells of the farmyard, she ended her days in a breaker's yard
on the River Clyde.

8   Crossing the Hard Way

Fresh from the bunkering berth, her once-smart paintwork blackened by coal dust, the British cargo vessel *Trevessa* slid clear of the breakwaters of the port of Fremantle, West Australia, and curtsied low as she felt the first push of the long Indian Ocean swell. It was Saturday 26 May 1923. Ahead of the *Trevessa* lay a challenging voyage of 11,500 miles, to the other side of the world. She was bound for Antwerp, with only a brief stop at Durban to replenish her bunkers.

Built in Germany in 1909 and owned by the Hain Steamship Company of London, the 5,004-ton *Trevessa* was, like all things Germanic, substantially constructed, and she was classed 100 A1 at Lloyd's, the highest registration class for a merchant ship. Her owners, part of the prestigious Peninsular & Oriental Group, had taken pains to see she was also equipped, maintained and manned to the best standards. Her master 36-year-old Captain Cecil Foster, was a seaman and navigator of considerable ability and experience. The *Trevessa* was then, in the common parlance of her day, a 'well-found' ship in all respects. Yet nine days after leaving Fremantle she radioed that she was sinking in mid-Indian Ocean. Ships answering her SOS reached the spot 2½ days later and found only scraps of wreckage and an upturned lifeboat. There was no sign of survivors.

Weeks passed with no news, and Captain Foster and his men joined the long list of those of their calling posted as lost at sea without trace. In towns and villages up and down the United Kingdom wives, mothers and girlfriends mourned and prepared to face a future suddenly made painfully empty. Then, on 27 June, twenty-three days after the *Trevessa*'s last plaintive message, from a lonely island in the South Indian Ocean came news of a miracle. A lifeboat containing Cecil Foster and seventeen of his crew had landed. These men, who had sailed a total of 1,700 miles in a twenty-six-foot boat, had a remarkable story to tell; a story of courage and endurance in the highest traditions of the British Merchant Navy.

When the *Trevessa* left Fremantle on 26 May, she was down to her maximum permissible marks with full bunkers, full fresh water and 6,500 tons of zinc concentrates in her holds. This cargo is loaded in a semi-liquid form, almost like wet cement, and is highly susceptible to shifting in heavy weather. Yet the possibility of the latter did not trouble Captain Foster unduly. If anything, he was more concerned with the state of his vessel's stability — that is, her ability to return to the upright when inclined by an outside force. By virtue of the heavy weight of concentrates at the bottom of her holds, the *Trevessa* had an excess of stability. In a seaway, she would have a quick, jerky roll, which is not only extremely uncomfortable but, over a long period, guaranteed to search out any hidden weaknesses in the ship's structure. Foster judged that the 4,500-mile passage to Durban, much of the time beam-on to the long rollers of the South Indian Ocean, would put a severe strain on both ship and men. He was uneasy.

For the first twenty-four hours out of Fremantle, there was blustery but fine weather. Then, on the 27th, the sky clouded over and the wind freshened from the south-south-west, becoming progressively stronger as the day wore on. By nightfall a full storm was raging, and for the next week the *Trevessa* laboured in a heavy beam swell, her tall masts and funnel tracing quick, erratic arcs against the ragged clouds, with every rivet in her hull groaning in protest.

On the morning of 3 June a mountainous sea rolled in and slammed into the port side of the ship, throwing spray high over the bridge. When the water receded, two of the *Trevessa*'s four lifeboats lay in ruins.

At around 22.00 that night, when the ship was hove-to and riding awkwardly with the wind and sea on the bow, she suddenly staggered as though she had run headlong into an unseen wall. Some said they heard an explosion, and a ripple of fear ran through the ship, for memories of the Great War were only five years old. Then the *Trevessa* recovered her stride, and it was assumed she had merely taken a particularly heavy sea bow-on.

By midnight it was obvious to Foster that his ship was in serious trouble. The seas were sweeping right over her foredeck, and each time she dipped, she seemed more and more reluctant to rise again.

Able Seaman Michael Scully, clawing his way forward at the change of the watch, heard the ominous swish of water as he drew abreast of No.1 hold. A less experienced man might have dismissed this as just another voice in the awful cacophony of the storm, but Scully, a shrewd Liverpudlian in his sixties, was quick to sense danger. He reported to the bridge, and Foster, accompanied by the chief engineer and carpenter, went forward to investigate.

It was as Scully had thought. No.1 hold was awash, with the water well above the height of the cargo. An inspection of the forepeak tank showed that the collision bulkhead – the specially strengthened watertight bulkhead in the eyes of the ship – was bulging inwards and in imminent danger of giving way.

Foster returned to the bridge and put the ship's head off the wind to ease the strain on the damaged bulkhead, then ordered the pumps onto No.1 hold. His efforts at containment were in vain, and by 01.00 on the 4th the seas were breaking green over the *Trevessa*'s forward hatches, as she settled slowly by the head. Fearing the worst, Foster issued lifejackets to all hands and ordered that the two remaining lifeboats be swung out ready for launching. At 04.16 he instructed his wireless-operator to begin sending out an SOS.

The distress call was heard by at least three ships, Shaw Savill & Albion's *Runic* and two other Hain Line steamers, the *Trevean* and *Tregenna*. Unfortunately the nearest of the three, the *Tregenna*, was 400 miles to the east, and all were in heavy weather and unable to increase speed.

Meanwhile, in the shrieking darkness of that terrible night, the *Trevessa*'s pumps were running hot and able to make little impression on the rising water in her forward hold. She was so far down by the head that her propeller was almost out of the water, and her foredeck was constantly awash. Foster knew it would be only a matter of time before her other watertight bulkheads collapsed and she went under, bow first.

The process of abandoning ship was not new to Cecil Foster. He had been twice torpedoed in the war, on the second occasion spending ten days in an open boat, suffering the agonies of thirst, hunger and exposure. He therefore laid his plans well, stocking the two lifeboats with extra water, cases of condensed milk, cigarettes, tobacco and sextants. At 02.15 he gave the order to abandon ship. The *Trevessa* was in position latitude 28°27′S, longitude 85°25′E, roughly 1,500 miles from the west coast of Australia.

In spite of the high seas threatening to smash them against the ship's side, the lifeboats got away safely, the only casualty being the ship's black Persian cat which, having been put in one of the boats, jumped back on board the *Trevessa* and was lost. It may have been that her feline intuition warned her of the ordeal in prospect for those in the boats and she preferred to die with the ship.

Captain Foster was in charge of one lifeboat, having nineteen men with him, while Chief Officer John Stewart-Smith took the other boat, with twenty-three men. Foster's boat nearly came to grief at the outset, when a huge wave lifted it right over the foredeck of the sinking ship. Luckily the receding waters carried it back again with only slight damage.

At 02.45 on 4 June, the *Trevessa*'s crew, forty-four men crammed into two tiny, storm-tossed lifeboats, watched sadly as the ship they had come to regard as their home slipped beneath the waves.

Cecil Foster was now faced with what was perhaps the most difficult decision of his life, for the *Trevessa* had gone down at one of the loneliest crossroads of the Indian Ocean. Australia lay 1,500 miles to the east, while the nearest land to the west was the island of Rodriguez, a small dot in the ocean and 1,600 miles away. To the south, 670 miles off, were the equally small islands of Amsterdam and St Paul; to the north there was nothing for 2,000 miles but the sweltering emptiness of the tropics.

The possibility of making for Amsterdam and St Paul Foster dismissed out of hand, for the islands were uninhabited and lay deep in the bitter cold and howling winds of the Roaring Forties. Likewise, he opted against sailing north, where the blazing sun would turn them into shrivelled corpses before land was reached. He could, of course, remain in the vicinity of the sinking and hope for rescue, but he knew this might take many days, during which the inactivity and cruel weather would destroy the morale of his men, eventually killing them as surely as if they had gone down with the ship. The temptation to try to make it back to Australia was very strong, but the wind and currents were against them. That left only Rodriguez, which they could posisbly reach by taking advantage of the south-east trade winds and the westerly flowing equatorial current. If they missed Rodriguez – and there was a distinct possibility they might, the island of Mauritius was only 300 miles further west; failing that, the shores of Madagascar lay beyond. To sail to the west was the only viable choice.

As a gesture to his would-be rescuers – if any – Foster held the boats riding to their sea anchors for the rest of that night and all next day. Except for the endless procession of angry waves, the horizon remained empty, and at sunset on the 4th the *Trevessa*'s boats hoisted sail and set out to the west.

The plan of action, worked out jointly by Foster and Stewart-Smith, was first to make to the north until the south-east trades were reached in about latitude 23°30′S, then north-west to latitude 19°30′S – the latitude of Rodriguez – and then due west to the island. They were following the old sailing-ship route, well trodden by their shellback forebears before them.

Due to the violent rolling and pitching of the small boats, the compasses proved useless but, steering by the sun and stars and checking their latitude by sextant whenever the opportunity occurred, they pushed northwards. Foster's boat, with a larger sail and lighter load, was by far the better sailer, and from time to time over the next five days he found himself forced to heave to while Stewart-Smith's boat laboriously narrowed the gap. On the morning of the 9th, after a bad night in which the two boats had had great difficulty in keeping in touch, Foster decided that it would be more sensible to part company. It was agreed that whoever was first to reach land would send help for the others.

Without the slower boat holding him back, Foster made good progress, despite the most appalling weather conditions, averaging about seventy miles a day. Then, on the 11th, the wind suddenly dropped away and for the next four days they were becalmed. Thanks to Foster's foresight, they still had a good supply of food and water but, ever conscious of the long voyage ahead, he had set the rations at a third of a cigarette tin of water, one biscuit and a few spoonfuls of condensed milk per day, per man. The men suffered most from thirst, even though, again benefiting from Foster's wartime experiences, they sucked buttons and pieces of coal to stimulate their saliva and kept their heads wet with salt water. The occasional shower of rain was a godsend, in which they bathed like excited children and collected water in tins and outstretched oilskins. But so weakened were they by hunger and the long battle with the sea that their morale had fallen to its lowest ebb. And there was worse to come.

By alternately rowing and drifting, they reached the southern boundary of the south-east trades on the afternoon of the 15th. A north-westerly course was then set and, with the wind right astern and freshening all the time, the ungainly lifeboat seemed to fly like a bird before the curling waves. But the kindly trade wind, so revered by the old windjammer men, proved to be a curse for the men crouching in their frail craft only inches above the sea. Moaning like a demented soul, the wind piled up the seas astern until they became pursuing white-topped mountains, hell-bent on the destruction of the boat. This torture went on day after day without let-up. Twice the boat was pooped and the exhausted men were forced to bail for their lives.

Under the cover of darkness, in spite of Foster's warning, some began to drink salt water and suffered the inevitable consequences. On 20 June Fireman Jacob Ali died, to be followed next day on his long voyage to the unknown by his shipmate Mussim Nazi. Their committal to the deep made more room in the crowded boat, but this was of little real comfort to those who remained. Foster was aware that the crucial stage in their ordeal had now been reached. As far as he could tell from sun sights, the boat was then in latitude 19°30′S and about 350 miles due east of Rodriguez. The consequences of missing the tiny island he refused to contemplate. They must press on.

On the morning of the 26th, a tremendous sea reared up astern and pounced on the boat, swamping it so that it sank to the gunwales. For the wretched survivors this final indignity must have offered the temptation to surrender and die quietly, but again they rallied and bailed. The reward for their efforts proved beyond price. At 14.45 as the half-waterlogged boat rose sluggishly on the crest of a wave, land was sighted. Five hours later, after narrowly escaping being wrecked on a reef, Foster and his men sailed into Port Mathurin, Rodriguez. They had covered almost 1,700 miles in twenty-two days and eighteen hours.

The second miracle occurred three days later, when Chief Officer John Stewart-Smith brought his boat into Baie du Cap, at the southern end of the island of Mauritius. They had missed Rodriguez and sailed a total of 2,200 miles in twenty-five days. The cost of Stewart-Smith's achievement was high. Four Arab firemen had succumbed through drinking sea-water; three Europeans, including one of the *Trevessa*'s young apprentices, had died of exposure, and Second Engineer David Mordecai had been lost overboard from the boat in a sudden squall.

The *Trevessa* lies in over a thousand fathoms of water, and the cause of her loss will never be known. Did she, on that dark, storm-filled night in June 1923, strike a submerged object – an old wreck floating just below the surface perhaps? Or was it a barnacle-covered mine, left over from the war and drifting unfulfilled in mid-ocean? This could account for the explosion said to have been heard. Or was it just the awesome power of the sea that smashed in the *Trevessa*'s bow and launched her crew on that long, hazardous voyage to the west?

9   Winter North Atlantic

The power of the sea is absolute. Never has this been more dramatically shown than in the North Atlantic in the winter of 1934. This was a season of storms of unparalleled ferocity and duration in an ocean renowned throughout the ages for its vile weather.

It was still autumn in British waters when the 4,860-ton cargo steamer *Ainderby* left Swansea on 21 September 1934. An area of high pressure was firmly established over Europe, giving cloudless skies and light winds, with only a hint of frost in the air presaging the approach of winter. The sea was calm as the *Ainderby* rounded Mumbles Head and pointed her bluff bows westwards. On the bridge her master, Captain Bestell, paced the freshly scrubbed boards, sniffing at the clean air, at peace with the world. After years of recession, when shipowners had fought over disappearing cargoes like hungry wolves, and men with masters' tickets stood in line for menial jobs on deck, British shipping was at last showing signs of sustained recovery. In consequence, the *Ainderby* was down to her marks with 8,000 tons of Welsh anthracite and bound for the Canadian port of Montreal. Admittedly the freight on this cargo was not high, but to Bestell and his crew, many of whom had been 'on the beach' in the bad days, the bulging holds spelled job security for many months to come.

Some 200 miles to the south-east, the equally heavily laden *Millpool* shouldered her way through the oily calm of the English Channel, also bound for Montreal. As he conned his ship past Beachy Head, its tall white cliffs shimmering in the coastal haze, Captain Newton, master of the *Millpool*, felt the tensions of the preceding four days slipping away. The passage from Danzig, where the *Millpool* had loaded a full cargo of grain, had been one fraught with all the dangers shallow and congested waters can

bring to a deep-laden ship. Now, with the busy Straits of Dover
safely astern, Newton was able to turn his mind to the 2,800-mile
voyage ahead. He was well aware that the long ocean crossing
might prove a serious challenge, for the ageing *Millpool*, built in
1906, was sagging noticeably under her heavy load. On the other
hand, he drew confidence from his long experience in the ways of
the sea, and the blessing of a first-class crew. The weather,
apparently set fair for some time to come, was an added bonus.

Given advantage of modern-day weather-forecasting, the
equanimity of the two master mariners might well have been
profoundly disturbed on that fine September day. Unknown to
them, the North Atlantic was already in the opening bars of a
mighty overture to winter. Far to the west, pressure was falling
rapidly over an area more than a thousand miles across, the
isobars were packing in and, urged on by the rising wind, the
surface of the great ocean had commenced to heave and roll with
a ponderous movement that spoke of its awesome power.

The *Ainderby* and the 4,218-ton *Millpool* were first cousins,
both out of the stable of Sir Robert Ropner & Co. of West
Hartlepool. They were typical tramp steamers of their day, being
small, underpowered and strictly functional. They might also be
described as forerunners of the modern bulk carrier, specifically
designed to carry coal, ores and grain to the maximum advantage.
To this end, they had large, unobstructed holds, topped by an
open shelter deck, which ran uninterrupted from forward to aft
and which, when piled with bulk cargo, acted as a gravity feeder
for the holds below. The cost of manual trimming in port was
therefore kept to a minimum, a very significant factor in those
days of low freights. Additionally, all cargo stowed in the shelter
deck was classed as being 'on deck' and attracted less in the way of
tonnage dues. In reality, this open deck, although intended as an
integral part of the ship's buoyancy, was an example of British
design at its worst. The deck had only two watertight bulkheads,
one at each end and forming part of the configuration of the well
decks. They were, therefore, completely exposed to the sea. In
heavy weather, the forward bulkhead inevitably took the full force
of the seas breaking over the bows. As an economic expedient, the
principle behind these ships was sound; to the men who sailed in
them, they were vulnerable ships, to be nursed with a firm but
delicate hand.

The *Ainderby* was the first to feel the force of the gathering

storm. Twenty-four hours out of Swansea, she ran into strong
south-westerly winds, accompanied by heavy rain and rising
seas. Soon her massive stem-bar was slamming into each
advancing wall of water with a force that threatened to shake
loose every rivet in her hull. Captain Bestell had no alternative
but to reduce speed.

For the next six days, the *Ainderby* struggled westwards,
fighting the sea for every precious mile gained. On the 28th she
was 600 miles to the west of Ireland and nearing the mid-point
in her ocean passage. To Bestell, his eyes heavy and face lined
with fatigue, the worst seemed to be over. Then the Atlantic,
which had really only been gathering its strength, struck with all
the spiteful, pent-up fury of a frustrated Goliath. The wind
came out of the west with hurricane force, and mountainous
seas thundered down on the *Ainderby*, slamming against her
bows and filling her well decks with boiling foam. Only by the
skilful use of helm and engines was Bestell able to prevent her
broaching-to.

Later that morning, when Bestell had finally succeeded in
heaving to with the wind and sea on the bow, the enraged
Atlantic claimed its first victim: 15-year-old Apprentice
Leonard Baxter was snatched from the deck by a wave and
swept overboard. Despite the danger of being caught beam-on
to the sea, Bestell immediately put the ship about and for three
long hours searched the heaving wastes in the vicinity of the
accident. His efforts were in vain. Leonard Baxter, youngest
member of the *Ainderby*'s crew, was never seen again.

Bestell was deeply saddened by the loss of the young boy, but
the professional code of the sea demanded he make every effort
to continue his voyage. Throughout the next three days, the
Ainderby lay bow-on to the wind and sea, barely making steerage
way and all the time weakening under the constant assaults of an
ocean gone berserk.

On the morning of 1 October hopes were raised by a gradual
moderation in the weather, and the battered tramp began to
forge slowly ahead towards the coast of Newfoundland, now less
than 500 miles off. Unfortunately the respite was short-lived. By
noon on the 2nd the storm clouds had regathered, the wind
began to shriek again and the sea resumed its angry attack.
Bestell was once again forced to reduce speed and then heave
to.

For more than two hours the *Ainderby* rode the sea, sliding awkwardly from crest to trough, uncomfortable, vulnerable but as safe as good seamanship could make her. Then, without warning, she slipped into a trough so deep that the sky was completely blotted out. Those on the bridge watched horror-stricken as a giant wave, its crest frothing white, reared up to mast-top height and then pounced with a triumphant roar. The *Ainderby* went down, groaning and shuddering under the weight of thousands of tons of green water, and it seemed she would never rise again. But rise she did, slowly and determinedly, shrugging aside the might of the great Atlantic. Her wounds, however, were grievous.

At the same time, 150 miles to the east, the *Millpool* was fighting her own lonely battle with the enraged ocean. On her bridge, a gaunt-faced Captain Newton managed a wry smile as he read the message handed to him by his wireless-operator: 'FROM S.S. AINDERBY 53°14′N 41°20′W. No. 1 HATCH FORWARD AND IRON BULKHEAD STOVE IN. BRIDGE PARTLY WIPED AWAY. CHIEF OFFICER INJURED. WE ARE UNABLE TO HEAVE TO.'

If anything, the *Millpool* was in an even more desperate situation than her cousin. Earlier in the day her forward hatch had been breached by the sea, and Newton had been obliged to turn and run before the storm. She was now heading back towards Ireland, down by the head through the water in her forward hold and riding the mountainous seas like a great, ungainly surfboat. As each sea raced up astern of her, filling the air with flying spray torn off its overhanging crest by a wind in excess of eighty knots, the ship was in constant danger of being overwhelmed. Yet, always at the last minute, it seemed, she was able to lift her old-fashioned stern high and ride up on the back of the wave and down into the following trough, her propeller racing and her decks streaming water. She was a brave ship, but Newton feared it must be only a matter of time before she faltered in her stride and stumbled in the path of the advancing seas.

The agony of the *Millpool* was not prolonged. A few hours later the American coast station, Mackay Radio picked up the following message: 'SOS ... FROM S.S. MILLPOOL 53°30′N 37°10′W. AFTER HATCH STOVE IN, MAIN TOPMAST GONE, THREE MEN INJURED. DRIVING HELPLESSLY BEFORE GALE. USING TEMPORARY AERIAL ... SOS.'

The plaintive cry for help was also heard by the *Ainderby*'s operator, but Bestell could offer Newton no more than his heartfelt sympathy, for his own ship was also in mortal danger. The rogue sea that had laid open the *Ainderby*'s No.1 hatch had also smashed the forward bulkhead of her shelter deck, so that she was wide open to the sea. Water had swept along the length of the shelter deck, cascading down into the holds and into the stokehold, threatening to douse the boiler fires. For a while it seemed the ship must go, swamped by the sea flooding unchecked through her hull; then, with a supreme effort, Bestell had brought her around so that she was stern on to the sea. Now, with her pumps working at full capacity and coping with the ingress, she was temporarily out of danger. Two ships, the Cunard liner *Antonia* and the cargo steamer *Trematon*, were standing by her. This gave some comfort to Bestell and his crew, but as seamen they were well aware that, should the *Ainderby* founder in such weather, the other ships could do little to save their lives.

Similar help was also on the way to the *Millpool*. Following her distress message, another Cunard liner, the *Ascania*, and the cargo ship *Beaverhill*, both eastbound across the Atlantic, were making all possible speed towards the position given by the stricken tramp. The *Ascania*, a ship of 14,000 tons, kept wireless contact with the *Millpool* throughout that day and into the night, but the distress signals grew fainter and fainter until at 02.00 (GMT) on the morning of 3 October they faded altogether.

The rescue ships reached the last position given by the *Millpool* just after dawn on the 3rd. They found only an empty expanse of angry sea. For the next twelve hours both ships, themselves at considerable risk in the huge seas, quartered the area, sending up rockets and calling on the *Millpool* to give her position. Nothing was seen or heard. At least a dozen other ships later joined in the search. They found nothing: no wreckage, no lifeboats, no bodies. The *Millpool* and her crew had disappeared off the face of the sea for ever.

To this day the fate of the *Millpool* and her twenty-six-man crew remains a mystery, but speculation as to how she met her end is not difficult. In her distress message she reported her main-topmast gone and her after hatch stove in, so it is highly probable that she was overtaken and pooped by a rogue wave similar in size to that which damaged the *Ainderby* – it may even have been the same wave. The consequences of being pooped would have been catastrophic, and in addition to the damage she declared, it is almost certain that the after bulkhead of the *Millpool*'s shelter deck caved in under the weight of water. The sea then had free access to the heart of the ship, destroying her reserve buoyancy, creating negative stability and possibly extinguishing her boiler fires. As she was already running before the storm, there was nothing Newton could have done to save her. She must simply have rolled over and been swallowed up by the sea.

The *Ainderby*, being slightly larger than the *Millpool* and younger by nineteen years, survived the terrible ordeal of the winter of 1934. She limped back into Swansea a week later, her decks and accommodation in a shambles, her deck plating cracked across the breadth of the ship amidships, and with a foot of water in her holds. Captain Bestell and his crew were tired, physically and mentally bruised, but unbeaten. Ten days later, after hurried repairs, they once more set out to challenge the North Atlantic. This time the *Ainderby* reached Montreal without mishap. Her end was not to come until seven years later, and then not by the hand of the sea but by a German torpedo. She still lies, along with so many of her kind, in a grave 120 miles to the north-west of Bloody Foreland.

The winter of 1934, which had begun with such sudden fury in that late September, raged in the North Atlantic almost unabated until the end of December, with violent storm following violent storm so closely that the ocean was forever in a frenzy. Apart from the *Millpool*, three other British tramps foundered with heavy loss of life, and reports of ships being swept by hundred-foot waves were common. These reports may have been subject to some exaggeration, but certainly the wave that hit the Japanese ship *Victoria Maru* in early December must have been a monster. When she staggered into Cardiff, her entire bridge superstructure and funnel had gone, along with her master, chief officer and third officer. The British ship *Monkleigh*, in difficulties 770 miles west of the Scillies, lost her mainmast and most of her deck cargo of timber and suffered severe damage to her superstructure. Ships were flung ashore on the Atlantic coasts of Spain and Portugal, and for almost three months cries for help jammed the wireless waves from Cape Hatteras to the Faroes and from Newfoundland to the Canaries.

10   And Again to War

The Second World War was only eleven days old when the British steamer *Truro* left the Firth of Forth, bound for the Norwegian port of Devanger, near Bergen. She was unarmed and carried no radio – an innocent participant in a war that was eventually to engulf half the civilized world and destroy the core of Britain's merchant fleet.

To 46-year-old Captain J.E. Egner, master of the *Truro*, the war to date had amounted to little more than a thoroughly unwarranted interference in his God-given mandate to command and navigate his ship in a manner dictated only by his experience and expertise. He had already felt the bureaucratic might of the Admiralty, having been ordered to call at the port of Methil to receive his routeing orders for the crossing of the North Sea. To a man who was as familiar with this sea as he was with his own back garden, this seemed an unnecessary waste of time, to say the least.

The 974-ton *Truro*, built at Aberdeen in 1922 and owned by Ellerman's Wilson Line of Hull, was only a tiny cog in the great wheel of the Ellerman shipping empire, whose trade routes stretched to the four corners of the globe. A bluff-bowed, overgrown coaster – as she was regarded by many, she was a regular trader between the east coast of Britain and ports in Scandinavia and the Baltic, covering the well-trodden path across the North Sea on a weekly basis. Her home port was Hull, Captain Egner and his crew of thirty-two lived in Hull, and more often than not she ended up in the Humber at the completion of each voyage. For Egner and his men this was a most satisfactory arrangement. However, as always, there was a price to be paid. In winter it was a hard run, with the North Sea often swept by fierce gales which churned this shallow sea into a frightening maelstrom, meting out savage punishment to the little *Truro* as she went about her business. Then, at the end of the outward passage, there was ice, snow and the bone-chilling cold that no multiple layers of clothing could keep at bay. The summer months were perhaps more comfortable but no less hazardous, for the curse of fog, dense and blinding, was frequently with them. Small, underpowered and equipped with the absolute minimum of navigational aids, the *Truro* was not a ship for the faint of heart at the best of times.

Having been duly briefed by the naval authorities, the *Truro* sailed from Methil at 14.00 on 14 September. Two hours later she had left the shelter of the Firth of Forth and was burying her bows in the first swells of the open sea. The weather was fine and clear, with no more than a fresh breeze, and Captain Egner was confident that the two-day passage to Norway would be an uneventful one. Methil had warned him to be on the lookout for U-boats, but he was inclined to think that the Navy was making a song and dance about nothing. In Egner's opinion, which he expressed to Second Officer Morrell, who stood beside him on the bridge as they headed out to sea, if the Germans had any sense, they would be out in the Atlantic looking for the big ships. In any case, the immediate enemy for the *Truro* was fog. There was, again in Egner's opinion, the smell of it in the air.

Egner was correct in his supposition that the Germans would be better occupied in the deep waters of the Atlantic. Unknown to him, the U-boats had, in fact, been out there in force since the third week in August, waiting for the signal to begin hostilities. When this came, they had wasted no time, sinking seventeen British merchantmen in the first ten days of the war. The situation in the North Sea was less threatening, the few U-boats operating in the area having found only one victim in that period.

The fog Egner had forecast did not materialize, neither did the enemy, and on the evening of the 15th the *Truro* was more than half-way across the North Sea, with just 120 miles to go to the Norwegian coast. As the sun dropped below the horizon and the long northern twilight began to draw its reassuring cloak around his small and vulnerable ship, Egner relaxed in his cabin.

On the bridge Chief Officer A.W. Johnson, who had the watch, paced the starboard wing, stopping occasionally to run his binoculars over the horizon. He too welcomed the coming of the night and was reassured by the fact that the *Truro* was apparently alone on an empty sea. Then he glanced astern and froze.

The frenzied shriek of the voicepipe whistle brought Egner tumbling out of his armchair. Seconds later, at Johnson's request, he was racing for the bridge ladder.

The submarine was about two miles off on the starboard quarter, trimmed down, and appeared to be shadowing them. Egner had no way of knowing if this was the enemy, but he was not in the mood to take chances. He brought his ship sharply round to the north, putting the submarine right astern, and called on the engine-room for maximum revolutions. His plan was simple – and, the *Truro* being unarmed, the only one open to him: he would run away, hoping to escape under the cover of darkness.

U-36, the *Truro*'s pursuer, was a Type II craft of 250 tons displacement, being in the eyes of the German Navy as insignificant as the *Truro* was to her big sisters who sailed the deep waters. She was one of Admiral Doenitz's original fleet of coastal submarines, built well before the outbreak of war and with a very limited operational range; hence her presence in the North Sea. For her commander, Kapitän-Leutnant Wilhelm Frolich, this was his first confrontation with the enemy, and he intended to play the game according to the rules laid down by the Prize Ordinance. (This unrealistic piece of international legislation, enacted by the League of Nations, stipulated that a submarine must first stop a merchant ship and allow her crew to take to the boats before sinking the ship.)

For the *Truro*, escape was, of course, impossible. The U-boat, running on the surface, had the legs of the small cargo ship, even though her firemen worked like men possessed to keep the boiler furnaces roaring. Steadily the distance separating pursuer and pursued shortened, and soon *U-36* was abeam to port of the *Truro*, her deck gun manned and pointing menacingly. Her signal lamp flashed the order to stop and abandon ship.

Grim-faced, Egner stared down the barrel of the U-boat's gun from his bridge. Given a gun of his own, however small, he would have been tempted to make a fight of it. Had he not fought the sea all his life, no matter how great the odds? But his cunning and navigational skills would be of little use against this enemy. He could conceivably continue to run, but sooner or later would come the hail of shells or the silent torpedo. The end result would only be more grieving widows, more fatherless children in the port of Hull. With a hopeless shrug, Egner walked into the wheelhouse and rang the engine-room telegraph to stop.

In order to gain precious time, Egner ordered Second Officer Morrell to contact the U-boat by semaphore, if possible feigning confusion and misunderstanding. Meanwhile he directed Chief Officer Johnson to stock the lifeboats with blankets, cigarettes, spirits and all the tinned food he could lay his hands on. Having no radio on board, he was unable to send an SOS, and there was no telling how long they might be adrift in the boats.

The U-boat was now signalling insistently for them to abandon ship, adding that the captain must bring all his papers with him when he left. Egner's answer to that was to gather up all his confidential papers and books and carry them below to the stokehold, where he tossed them into the dying flames of a boiler furnace.

With the shadows of night drawing swiftly in, the *Truro*'s two lifeboats were lowered, Egner taking the starboard boat and Johnson the port one. The evacuation was orderly and unhurried, but there was a moderate swell running, and Egner's boat was slammed against the ship's side and slightly damaged. The only casualty was the *Truro*'s chief engineer, who bruised his ribs when falling from the deck of the ship into the sea.

As Egner's boat pulled around the bow of the *Truro*, the U-boat came into full view. She was about 150 feet in length, with a small but deadly-looking gun on her fore casing and a large instrument abaft the conning tower resembling a range-finder. There were no rust streaks on her grey paint, and her only identifying mark was a red swastika painted on the side of her conning tower. While Egner was mentally photographing the enemy, Morrell, who was in the same boat, was busy with his camera, making a more permanent record of the submarine's appearance. Fortunately for him, the Germans did not appear to notice his activity.

The submarine now hailed the lifeboats, asking the captain to come aboard with his papers. Egner, suspicious, yet curious to meet the man who was holding his ship at gunpoint, ordered his men to pull for the U-boat. The only papers he carried with him were the ship's articles and certificates, which could hardly be regarded as being of a secret nature.

The boat bumped alongside the after end of the submarine, and Egner, clutching his bundle of papers, was helped aboard by two German seamen. He was then escorted to the conning tower, where he came face to face with Wilhelm Frolich, a man in his early thirties with a sallow complexion and several days' growth of beard on his chin. Frolich was polite, almost apologetic, when he explained to Egner that it would be necessary to sink his ship. Not expecting anything less, Egner shrugged and handed over his papers. No one would be more aggrieved than he at the sinking of the *Truro*.

Frolich gave the papers a cursory examination and then handed them back to Egner. He enquired if the captain had sent out an SOS and was somewhat surprised when Egner admitted that his ship did not carry a radio. The conversation became less strained, and it was Egner's turn to be surprised when the German asked for his help in fixing the submarine's position, which had been in some doubt for two days past. Having personally taken sun sights earlier in the day, Egner took a great delight in giving the German Navy a lesson in navigation.

Egner was now invited, not ordered, to enter the submarine, but it was with some misgiving that he lowered himself through the conning-tower hatch and climbed down into the control-room. He had heard rumours that the Germans were in the habit of making prisoners of ships' captains. Was he to end up in a prisoner-of-war-camp?

Whatever the Germans' intentions, they showed no animosity towards Egner. It seemed that the whole crew of the U-boat – twenty-five or thirty men – had crowded into the control-room, agog with curiosity. They were all young, fresh-faced and eager to try out their limited English on the bewildered ship-master. He was not to know that this was their first sight of the enemy, *U-36* having, until then, been in contact only with neutral Norwegian ships. While answering the questions fired at him, Egner gained confidence and took the opportunity to look around him, taking careful note of the layout of instruments and equipment. The Admiralty would welcome any such information – should he be allowed to go free.

When they returned to the conning tower, Frolich expressed a genuine regret that his country should be involved in a war with Britain, a sentiment with which Egner heartily agreed. As seamen, neither could see sense in the wanton sinking of ships which the war would undoubtedly demand. The bond between the two men became firmer. They exchanged names and addresses, agreeing that they should meet after the war, which Frolich confidently forecast would not last more than another two months. Without prompting, the commander now offered to use the U-boat's radio to send out an SOS, so that the *Truro*'s lifeboats would not be long adrift before help came. Egner accepted gratefully and asked for additional water for the boats. As the U-boat was short of water herself, Frolich could offer only two dozen bottles of beer. They were handed down to the waiting survivors, who accepted them with acclamation. A bucket was also lowered to Egner's damaged boat to help with the bailing.

Feeling that the situation had become completely detached from the realities of war, Egner shook hands with Frolich and made to leave the conning tower. As he put his foot on the first rung of the ladder, a heavy hand on his shoulder stopped him. In a complete reversal of his previous attitude, Frolich now informed Egner that he was to be made prisoner and taken back to Germany.

The dumbfounded Egner at once refused to stay, pointing out that his place was in the boats with his men. A heated argument between the two captains followed, but in the end Frolich relented. He agreed to release the Britisher if he would sign a paper declaring he would not go to sea again until the war was over. The prospect of such an undertaking, which had a Napoleonic ring to it, did not appeal to Egner. He pointed out to Frolich that he was a master mariner and could not, under any circumstances, give up his profession. But the commander was adamant. If Egner did not sign the paper, he would be taken as a prisoner of war. Frolich now also demanded that the *Truro*'s chief and second officers be brought aboard to sign the same declaration.

Johnson and Morrell were called aboard the submarine and clambered up into the cramped conning tower, mystified but curious. Frolich once more explained the terms under which all three could gain their parole and produced a printed document, which he translated from the German and offered to the two men for signature. The two officers flatly refused to sign, and for a while it seemed that the entire navigation department of the *Truro* would be whisked off into captivity. Then Egner made a quick decision. The whole thing was so ridiculous as to be laughable. No one could ever hold them to a promise of this nature made under duress. Furthermore, the document Frolich offered was in German, a language which he and his officers could not understand. With a slight shrug of his shoulders he signed, indicating to the others to do likewise. Surprisingly, Frolich accepted the sudden surrender without question, and after a final handshake all round, Egner took his officers back to the lifeboats.

As the boats were pulling clear of the submarine, Egner heard a muffled thump and knew his ship was doomed. Silently he watched the torpedo feather its way across the intervening water to explode with a flash and an angry roar, tearing open the *Truro*'s defenceless hull midway between her No.2 and 3 holds.

The little ship, a survivor of seventeen years of the worst that Europe's northern seas could throw at her, did not die easily. Frolich manned his deck gun and opened fire but, even though the range was less than half a mile, only one hit was scored. The German commander was then forced to use another of his precious torpedoes to finish the job. The torpedo ran true, hitting the *Truro* in way of her boiler-room. She blew up and sank within two minutes.

Having disposed of the British ship, Wilhelm Frolich now showed amazing compassion to her crew. He called the two lifeboats back alongside and informed Egner that he had sent out an SOS, using the *Truro*'s call sign. Until help came, he would take the boats in tow. And so they set off, the U-boat motoring quietly on the surface, the lifeboats strung out behind on a long tow line, for all the world like a mother hen leading her chicks to safety.

After about half an hour Frolich stopped and allowed the boats to come up to him. He pointed out the lights of a ship to port and fired a series of red distress flares to attract the unknown vessel's attention. When he felt he had done so, the German commander wished Egner and his men good luck, cast off the tow rope and motored off into the night.

As soon as the U-boat was out of sight, swallowed up in the darkness, Egner turned his attention to the approaching ship, which, as it was showing lights, he assumed to be neutral. The lifeboat distress flares were broken out and burned, but although the ship came within two miles of the boats and could hardly have failed to see the flares, it did not stop. The rest of the horizon was empty as far as the eye could see, and Egner realized he must now attempt to sail the boats back to the British coast. The nearest point, the coast in the region of Aberdeen, was about 115 miles away, forty-eight hours' sailing, if the weather did not deteriorate – and there was no guarantee of that.

The two boats sailed westwards throughout the remainder of the night, steering by their dimly lit compasses and striving to keep in sight of each other. At about 08.30 on the 16th, an aircraft passed low over the water, about five miles away. Not knowing, or caring, whether the plane was friend or foe, the survivors stood up in the boats, shouting and waving. But it was no good. The aircraft continued serenely on its course, giving no sign that the boats had been sighted.

The sun climbed towards its zenith, and still the sea around them remained stubbornly empty. The complete absence of fishing-trawlers worried Egner, for this part of the North Sea was normally well populated by fishermen. He began to wonder if they had all run for shelter before an advancing gale; it was most unlikely that the weather would hold fair for much longer. Then, in the late afternoon, smudges of smoke were sighted on the horizon to the west, and it seemed they had found the fishing-fleet at last.

Darkness fell on this the second day of their ordeal, but although they sailed steadily westwards, the reassuring pencils of smoke drifting skywards from the horizon came no nearer. The night dragged on; they were cold and tired, and morale was flagging. Midnight passed, and the next day, Sunday, was upon them when, suddenly, they found themselves among a fleet of trawlers.

Egner galvanized his men into action. The oars were shipped and the boats pulled hard for the nearest trawler, burning distress flares as they went. To their complete surprise, the fisherman put his stern to them and made off at speed like a frightened rabbit. The same thing happened time and time again as the boats, burning their rapidly diminishing stock of flares, attempted to approach the nearest trawler. The farce was rapidly turning into a tragedy, for it was obvious to Egner that the fishermen had mistaken his boats for the enemy and were in mortal fear of being stopped. There remained only one solution.

If the fishermen would not voluntarily rescue them, they must be made to do so.

Egner consulted Johnson, and they each selected a trawler to shadow and approach silently – no shouts, no flares. It was hard, painstaking work, but the plan succeeded and two Belgian trawlers suddenly found themselves boarded by a gang of dirty, unshaven and desperate British seamen, who must have put the fear of God into them. Fortunately there was no violence, and when the *Truro*'s survivors had explained their predicament to the Belgians, they were treated with great kindness. Egner and his men were landed in Aberdeen later that day, having spent thirty-three hours in the lifeboats.

The crew of the *Truro* were early victims of a war at sea that had not yet degenerated into a vicious killing-match. In Wilhelm Frolich they had met with a U-boat commander who, although dedicated to taking the war to Germany's enemies, did so with compassion and regard for human life. In the years that were to follow, there were few of his kind in evidence.

Following her meeting with the *Truro*, *U-36* sank the Swedish steamer *Silesia* off the coast of Norway on 25 September, but that was to be her last victory. Two months later she was sunk in the North Sea by His Majesty's submarine *Salmon*. Her war had been a short and unproductive one.

11   The Fugitive

As the Second World War progressed, Axis naval sources estimated that, in order to bring Britain to her knees, they required to sink 700,000 tons of Allied merchant shipping per month over a long period. By the end of October 1942 they were very near to reaching their goal, having sunk ninety-three ships of more than 600,000 tons. The great majority of these sinkings took place in the Atlantic and were almost certainly a direct result of a shortage of escorts for Allied ships. At that time 'Operation Torch', the invasion of North Africa, was under way, with simultaneous landings at Algiers, Oran and Casablanca planned, involving some 800 merchant ships sailing in convoys from British and American ports. The protection of these convoys was a massive operation which stretched Allied naval and air forces to their utmost limits. Any Allied merchant ship not involved in this gigantic seaborne attack was more than likely to find herself sailing alone and protected only by God and the strength of her own arms. One such was the Glasgow ship *Empire Glade*.

The sun had just risen over Table Bay when, at 06.00 on 6 November 1942, the *Empire Glade* passed through the breakwaters of Cape Town harbour and lifted easily on the long rollers of the South Atlantic. The coolness of the African night was still in the air, but the cloudless blue sky presaged yet another glorious summer day. On the bridge of the ship, Captain George Duff felt the first warmth of the sun on his neck and thought briefly, and without regret, of his native Liverpool, 6,000 miles away and, inevitably at this time of the year, cold, sunless and shrouded in fog. He gave an involuntary shiver and turned his thoughts to the voyage ahead. The *Empire Glade* was bound in ballast for the island of Trinidad, where she would load whatever cargo the Ministry of War Transport had scheduled for her. Duff had not yet been let into this secret, but he had no worries about the passage across the South Atlantic. The weather was likely to be favourable, and he had complete confidence in his ship and crew.

The *Empire Glade* was a motor vessel of 7,006 tons, built in 1941 at the Barclay Curle yard on the Clyde for the Ministry of War Transport. Being a replacement ship designed to fill one of the many gaps in Britain's merchant fleet left by an increasingly active enemy, she had been built in a hurry. That is not to say that she was shoddily built, but she was somewhat basic in construction. Managed and manned for the ministry by the Blue Star Line of London, she was commanded by 42-year-old Captain George Duff and carried a crew of forty-eight which included six naval gunners seconded to the ship under the Defensively Equipped Merchant Ships (DEMS) arrangement. Her top speed was twelve knots, and she mounted a 4-inch anti-submarine gun and a 12-pounder aft, while her bridge and boat deck bristled with six machine-guns and four rocket-launchers. She also carried three depth-charges on a ramp at her stern, which must have been no more than a morale-booster, for to have dropped these even at her best speed of twelve knots would most likely have blown her stern off.

Despite the *Empire Glade*'s show of arms, Captain Duff's confident approach to the coming voyage might have been dented had he known of the enemy's activities in the Western Atlantic. A powerful group of U-boats, consisting of *U-67*, *U-129*, *U-156*, *U-161* and *U-502*, had moved in to cover the south-eastern approaches to the United States and the Caribbean. A net had been cast which could prove deadly for unsuspecting Allied ships.

On the morning of 8 November the *Empire Glade* was almost 600 miles north-west of Cape Town and making good progress in fine weather. At the same time, some 4,000 miles to the north, events which would effect the Blue Star Ship's future were moving swiftly to a climax. Shortly before dawn on that day, 290,000 American and British troops landed on the beaches of Casablanca, Algiers and Oran and within hours were advancing inland. It was the beginning of the end for Rommel and the Afrika Corps. Already merchant ships loaded to the gunwales with military stores needed to sustain the advance were queuing up off the beachheads, and many more such ships would be needed throughout the coming months.

Far on the other side of the world, close northwards of the island of Trinidad, a drama on a smaller scale was taking place. The ex-Italian, British-manned steamer *Capo Olmo* had been torpedoed by *U-67* and was damaged and struggling to make good her escape. This she did. As a result, the frustrated commander of *U-67*, Korvetten-Kapitän Günther Muller-Stockheim, decided to try his luck further out in the Atlantic, where, through the changing course of events, his path would eventually cross that of the *Empire Glade*.

The *Empire Glade* crossed the Equator on the 23rd in the region of St Paul Rocks, a barren, uninhabited archipelago lying 550 miles off the coast of Brazil. The weather continued fine, and in the absence of any reports of U-boat activity, George Duff still had high hopes of an uneventful passage.

Four days later, on the night of the 27th, Duff was on the bridge writing up his night orders when the radio officer handed him a message form. This contained instructions from the Admiralty diverting the *Empire Glade* to Charleston, South Carolina, to which she was to proceed with all despatch to load cargo. The Allies' North African adventure was in urgent need of more supplies.

At 04.00 on the 28th Chief Officer Glyn Roberts took over the watch from Second Officer Francis Hender. The ship was 640 miles east-north-east of Barbados and zigzagging around a mean course of 320°. Having checked compass, chart and log-book, Roberts chatted to Hender for a few minutes and then bade him goodnight. Hender, who would be back on the bridge for morning sights at 09.00, wasted no time in going below to his bunk. When he had gone, Roberts poured himself a second mug of hot, strong tea and wandered out into the wing of the bridge.

It was quiet in the wing, with only the quick, muted beat of the *Empire Glade*'s diesel engine breaking the silence. The weather had deteriorated a little, the moon struggling to pierce a thick overcast, and showers were blanketing sections of the horizon. However, the wind remained light, and only a slight sea and low swell were running. Roberts anticipated a peaceful watch.

In the engine-room Second Engineer Dugald Kinleyside had

the watch and was also on his second mug of tea. When that was drained, he would begin his customary round of the main engine and auxiliaries. For the moment, he drank and listened to the pulsating machinery around him. It all sounded as sweet as his tea.

Right aft, in the cramped, airless crew's quarters, cabin boy Leonard Prestidge slept lightly, carried on the wings of a dream back to his home overlooking the estuary of the River Dee. At sixteen, Prestidge had the world at his feet and was content.

On the poop deck, the DEMS gunners on watch sipped steaming mugs of Navy-issue cocoa and quartered the dark horizon with questioning eyes. Their whispered talk – it was a night for whispers – was of North Africa and of those less fortunate than themselves who were caught up in the fighting war. Out here, in the broad reaches of the Atlantic, where only the threshing of the *Empire Glade*'s propeller below their feet disturbed the night, the angry crack of gunfire and the screams of the wounded and dying seemed so far away.

But the ocean was not as empty as it seemed. Nine miles ahead of the *Empire Glade*, hidden in a passing rain squall, a long, low shape lurked on the water. *U-67*, having sunk three ships since damaging the *Capo Olmo* on the 8th, was lying in wait for another victim.

At 04.50 the *Empire Glade* completed the last leg of her current zigzag pattern, and Roberts steadied her on course before commencing the next pattern. As he turned away from the compass, there was a bright flash fine on the starboard bow, followed by the sharp crack of a gun; seconds later a shell whistled overhead. In this the darkest hour before the dawn, the *Empire Glade* was under attack.

In his cabin directly below the bridge, Captain Duff lay fully dressed on his day-bed, dozing but, as always, subconsciously alert. He was on his feet and rushing for the bridge ladder almost before the sound of the gun had died away. He reached the bridge as the unseen gun crashed out again but, as on the first occasion, the shell again overshot the ship and exploded harmlessly in the sea to port.

A third shell followed, and this found its mark in the *Empire Glade*'s forward rigging. The wireless aerials came down – no doubt achieving the primary object of the shell; one of the liferafts carried in the rigging was shattered by the blast, and a container of red distress flares in the raft was set alight. The ship was suddenly bathed in a brilliant red glow which must have been visible from horizon to horizon.

George Duff felt like a small, defenceless animal caught in the headlights of an approaching car. He had no forward mounted guns with which to retaliate, and with his ship giving a good imitation of a Roman candle, it would be useless to turn and run. There was only one possible alternative, and he took it without hesitation. Bringing the gun flashes right ahead, Duff gave a double ring on the engine-room telegraph, indicating that he required emergency full speed ahead.

U-67's gunners continued to fire at a rapid rate, the illuminated *Empire Glade* obviously presenting them with a perfect target. Their fourth shot struck the forward end of the ship's bridge, exploding in the cabin Duff had recently vacated. The explosion severed the voice-pipe which provided the only communication between the bridge and engine-room and, by some terrible quirk of fate, also damaged the electrical wiring leading to the morse signalling lamp high up on the signal mast. The bright white light came on and stayed on, despite all efforts to extinguish it. The *Empire Glade*, flares still burning in her rigging, could not have been better illuminated.

With the shells falling all around his ship at the rate of one every ten seconds, Duff was forced to come to terms with his predicament. If he persisted in his attempt to ram the attacker, the *Empire Glade* would surely be blown out of the water within the next few minutes. But he had no intention of giving up the fight. Stopping only to hurl the ship's confidential books overboard in their specially weighted box, he ordered the helm hard to port. It was time to bring his guns to bear.

As the cumbersome merchant ship answered slowly to her helm, swinging in a wide circle, she ran the gauntlet of a fusillade of shells fired by *U-67*. She was repeatedly hit in the hull and superstructure, and one shell slammed into her engine-room. Kinleyside, who had by this time been joined by Chief Engineer John Parker, was thrown to the plates by the blast, and both men narrowly escaped injury by shrapnel. So savage and deadly had the attack become that Duff was forced to consider saving the lives of his crew before it was too late. Reluctantly he rang the engine-room telegraph, and the frenzied beat of the engine slowed and then died away.

By this time the *Empire Glade*'s stern had swung around far enough for her 4-inch gun to bear. The gun's crew, led by Second Officer Hender and Gunlayer Turner, lost no time in opening fire, using the flashes of the other gun as a target.

On the bridge, George Duff, encouraged by the sound of his own gun hitting back, had second thoughts about abandoning the ship. However, Parker and Kinleyside, under the impression that the ship was sinking, had by now shut down the engine and come on deck, intending to go to their boat stations. Duff called Parker to the bridge and advised the chief that he had a mind to make a run for it. Without hesitation, Parker volunteered to go below and restart the engine. He was followed down the ladder by Kinleyside, and seven minutes later the *Empire Glade* was once more under way and working up to full speed. Duff put the enemy's gun flashes right astern and steadied the ship on a course that would take her away from the danger as rapidly as possible.

There was a last exchange of fire between the two ships, the U-boat lobbing two more shells wide to starboard of the fleeing merchantman, whose 4-inch replied with four rounds. The liferaft flares had at last burned out, and with her signal lamp extinguished, the *Empire Glade* made off into the darkness, using every revolution Parker and Kinleyside could coax from her engines.

It was by now 05.25, and the paling of the horizon to the east indicated that the *Empire Glade* would soon lose the cover of the night. It was Gunlayer Turner who suggested they try using smoke floats to cover their escape. As dawn broke, two floats were put over the stern, creating a most effective screen, behind which the ship was able to escape in a south-westerly direction, keeping to the windward edge of the smoke.

The fierce action with *U-67* had lasted just over half an hour, during which time Duff estimated the enemy had fired between twenty and thirty shells at his ship, scoring eight hits in all. An inspection of the damage showed five holes in the starboard side of the hull – all fortunately above the waterline – and extensive but not serious damage to the superstructure. In human terms, five men had been slightly injured, and sadly the youngest member of the crew, 16-year-old cabin boy Leonard Prestidge, had been killed. He was buried in the lonely deeps of the Atlantic, 3,000 miles from the land that bore him.

Taeping with *Fiery Cross*

HMS *Birkenhead* breaking up off Danger Point

SS *Great Western* sets off for New York

Brussels leaving port, outward bound for the Hook of Holland

Captain Foster's mementoes, including the ship's sextant, spoon and comb used aboard the lifeboat. Auctioned at Cardiff in 1988

Captain Foster (left) and Chief Officer Smith of the *Trevessa*

Pacific Charger aground off Baring Head
(WELLINGTON EVENING POST)

Ondina's gun crew, including Second Officer Bakker (back row, third from right) and AB Hammond (front row, far right)

The broken halves of the *Samtampa* lying off Sker Point

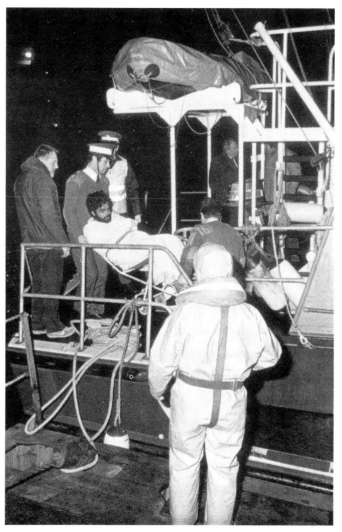

A Guernsey lifeboat lands survivors off *Radiant Med*
(GUERNSEY EVENING POST)

Stern section of *Texaco Caribbean*

Captain David
McCaffrey of
Caribbean Breeze

Having tended his wounded and buried his dead, George Duff turned his attention to the repair of his ship, for she was still more than 2,000 miles from her destination. For the next forty-eight hours a team of men led by Chief Officer Roberts worked day and night to patch the holes in the ship's side. It was due largely to their efforts that the *Empire Glade* reached Charleston on the night of 7 December.

Some well-deserved medals were handed out when the *Empire Glade*'s story was finally told. Captain George Duff received the George Medal and Lloyd's War Medal for Bravery at Sea. Chief Engineer John Parker was awarded the OBE, while Chief Officer Glyn Roberts, Second Officer Francis Hender and Second Engineer Dugald Kinleyside received the MBE. In addition, the ship's carpenter, Harry Shakeshaft, and the engine-room storekeeper, Frank Simmonds, were given the BEM (British Empire Medal) in recognition of their unflagging efforts to repair the ship.

There were no medals for *U-67*. Following her unsuccessful brush with the *Empire Glade*, she was to sink no more ships in this war. On 16 July 1943 she was caught on the surface in the North Atlantic by aircraft from the US carrier *Core* and sent to the bottom.

12   The Eleventh Hour

On the morning of 11 November 1942, while flags around the cenotaphs of a beleaguered Britain dipped in homage to those who had made the supreme sacrifice, two ships, one British and one Dutch, prepared for battle in the lonely reaches of the South Indian Ocean. Theirs was not to be a day of glory, of creaming bow-waves and thundering broadsides, but a desperate struggle for survival against impossible odds.

The 14,000-ton Dutch tanker *Ondina* had sailed from Fremantle on 5 November, escorted by the 650-ton Royal Indian Navy minesweeper *Bengal*, bound for the Indian Ocean island of Diego Garcia. Commanded by Captain Willem Horsman and manned by Dutch officers and Chinese ratings, the *Ondina* was armed with a single 4-inch gun mounted on her poop. Her gun's crew, led by Able Seaman Herbert Hammond RANR was made up of four Royal Navy ratings, three Royal Artillery gunners and a Dutch merchant seaman gunner. The *Bengal*, dwarfed by her huge charge, was commanded by Lieutenant-Commander William Wilson RINR and carried British officers and Indian ratings. She had a top speed of twelve knots, and her sole armament consisted of a 12-pounder gun mounted forward. For this gun she had on board only forty rounds of ammunition.

Lieutenant-Commander Wilson was not unduly concerned with his lack of firepower as he pressed north-westwards, the *Ondina* dutifully keeping station astern of him. By the autumn of that year the Indian Ocean had been largely cleared of German surface raiders. A few U-boats were reported operating in the southern approaches to the Mozambique Channel, but that was more than 2,000 miles to the west of the small convoy's proposed route. As for the Japanese, after a determined and very bloody foray against Allied shipping in the early summer, using armed merchant cruisers and submarines, they had long since retired sated to their bases in Malaya. Wilson's only other potential enemy, the weather, had also sheathed its claws. In November the Indian Ocean is free of cyclones and under the benign influence of the north-east monsoon, which brings with it a season of cloudless blue skies and zephyr-like winds. However, for a small ship like the *Bengal*, the 2,800-mile passage to Diego Garcia would be no mean feat of endurance. Wilson, although he would have been loath to admit as much, drew great comfort from the presence of the big merchantman lumbering along in his wake.

On board the *Ondina*, Captain Horsman was in a similarly contented frame of mind. Apart from 390 tons of fuel oil much of it needed to refuel the *Bengal* from time to time, he had nothing more volatile in his cargo tanks than salt-water ballast. For a man used to the awesome burden of commanding over the carriage of thousands of tons of high-octane gasoline, this was a pleasant relief indeed. At his tiny escort Horsman cast a somewhat jaundiced eye. The *Bengal* seemed no bigger than the average North Sea trawler, and in the event of a meeting with the enemy, her 12-pounder pea-shooter would probably prove a very empty threat. But, puny though she might be, the *Bengal* had about her the tight, resolute air of a British man-of-war. Horsman could not help being impressed.

At 11.00 on the 11th, the two ships were making ten knots and in position 20°S, 93°E, just over the half-way mark on their long passage. The weather was fine, the sun hot in a clear, blue sky, and the sea like a mirror, its glassy surface disturbed only by the ships' bow waves and occasional darting shoals of flying fish. This was the Indian Ocean at its idyllic best.

On the bridge of the *Bengal*, which was keeping station a quarter of a mile ahead of the *Ondina*, the officer of the watch lifted his binoculars and made a slow sweep of a horizon as sharp as a whetted knife. At 10° on the port bow he snapped alert. The masts and funnel of a large ship were just lifting above the horizon. He dived for the captain's voice-pipe.

Wilson was on the bridge within seconds and reaching for his own binoculars. Following the pointing finger of the officer, he brought the glasses to his eyes and swore softly. The ship, now hull up, was a large one – about 10,000 tons, he estimated – and she had the lines of a passenger vessel. In this time and place that could mean only one thing – an armed merchant cruiser. Wilson knew she was unlikely to be British.

The unknown ship was heading straight for the *Bengal* and *Ondina* and closing on them rapidly. At eight miles Wilson's worst fears were confirmed. The short, unraked funnel, clipper bows and cruiser stern were all unmistakeably Japanese. A few minutes later he was able to make out the funnel markings of the Nippon Yusen Kaisha (NYK) Line. No further proof was needed.

Wilson's next actions were quick and decisive. Ordering hands to battle stations, he altered course 90° to starboard away from the approaching enemy, at the same time signalling the *Ondina* to take up position on his starboard beam. No sooner had the *Bengal* put herself between the enemy and the tanker than a second ship came over the horizon, hard on the heels of the first. Wilson's face went white under his tan as he once again lifted his binoculars and identified the funnel colours of the NYK.

Although Wilson was not aware of it at the time, he was facing the Japanese raiders *Hokoku Maru* (10,438 tons) and *Aikoku Maru* (10,500 tons). Both vessels carried ten 5.9-inch guns, torpedo tubes and spotter aircraft.

On identifying the second ship as a belligerent, Wilson ordered the *Ondina* to reverse her course and make off to the south-east at maximum speed, giving her a rendezvous to keep twenty-four hours later, should both ships still be afloat – and at the time this must have seemed extremely unlikely. He then turned the *Bengal* to face the *Hokoku Maru* and increased to full speed. The diminutive David was rushing to challenge a Goliath more than fourteen times his size.

Perhaps unable to comprehend such audacity, the commander of the *Hokoku Maru* held his fire until the two ships were only 3,500 yards apart and still closing. When the Japanese did open up, her first shell landed 400 yards ahead of the *Bengal*. The British ship's small gun spat back defiantly, but the range was far too great for accuracy.

The *Aikoku Maru* now entered the fight, and the sea around the tiny minesweeper became a maelstrom of bursting shells. Yet, by some miracle, the *Bengal* was not hit and stood on, weaving from side to side like the fly-weight she was, but always her bow coming back to face the *Hokoku Maru*. Her gun's crew, all Indian ratings, crouched behind the thin shield of the 12-pounder, loading, laying and firing with determination and precision. Above them, on the bridge, Lieutenant-Commander Wilson and his officers settled their steel helmets firmly and steadied themselves against the frantic vibration set up by the *Bengal*'s racing engine. There would be no turning back.

When he received orders from the *Bengal* to proceed independently, Captain Horsman of the *Ondina* was thereby relieved of all responsibility in the action, other than that of saving his own ship. But Horsman, marvelling at the bravery of the British ship as she rounded on the Japanese like a snarling terrier, decided that this was one fight he could not stay out of. His ship was not equipped for an offensive role, but Horsman was confident she could still play her part in the battle and at the same time, perhaps, save herself.

Instead of altering course 180° and running away from the scene, as instructed by Wilson, Horsman came around only 90°, presenting his stern and already manned 4-inch to the *Hokoku Maru*. He did not increase speed. At 8,000 yards, Horsman gave the order to open fire. On the poop Second Officer Bartele Bakker, officer in charge of the gun, tapped the shoulder of Able Seaman Hammond, who was already crouched over his sight. The 4-inch barked and recoiled.

The *Ondina*'s first shell screamed over the *Hokoku Maru* to explode 400 yards astern of her. Hammond adjusted the range, and the next three shots landed short of their target. The fifth shell scored a direct hit on the after deck of the Japanese raider, causing a violent explosion and hurling the debris of her two aircraft high in the air. A fierce fire, probably fuelled by high-octane petrol, was seen to break out.

The *Hokoku Maru*, still trading shell for shell with the pugnacious *Bengal*, now turned some of her guns on the *Ondina*. Within minutes the tanker was hit, one of her lifeboats being smashed and her main topmast and wireless aerials brought crashing down. Shells fell all around her, throwing up a curtain of spray that obscured the aim of the 4-inch crew. Hammond, showing remarkable coolness, waited for the spray from each salvo to clear before firing his own gun. In this way he registered five hits in succession on the raider, the fifth shell again striking her after deck and setting off an even more massive explosion, which appeared to demolish much of her stern section.

The *Hokoku Maru* stopped and began to settle by the stern, but her guns continued to fire.

From the *Bengal*, under fire from both raiders but still unharmed, a great cheer went up at the crippling of the *Hokoku Maru*. It was thought the *Bengal*'s 12-pounder had caused the damage, for in the heat of the battle it had not been noticed that the *Ondina* had disobeyed orders and weighed in with her 4-inch. There is no evidence to confirm which gun caused the explosion on the *Hokoku Maru* – presumably her magazine was hit – but it seems likely that the heavier shells of the *Ondina*'s 4-inch were responsible.

Wilson, even if he had been so inclined, had no time to apportion credit for the victory. Shells were bursting all around the *Bengal*, and inevitably she was soon hit repeatedly and on fire herself. Wilson was now faced with the critical decision of whether to go on or pull back. His ship had received considerable punishment and, with only five rounds left for the 12-pounder, would soon be defenceless. For the first time since joining the action with the Japanese, Wilson now looked around for the *Ondina*. To his great relief, she had opened up the distance between herself and the raiders to about seven miles and appeared to be escaping to the south-east undamaged. He decided to break off the engagement and retire under the cover of a smoke-screen while his ship was still afloat.

The *Aikoku Maru* gave chase – as Wilson had hoped she would – and for a further fifteen minutes continued to fire on the minesweeper. Then she also gave up the fight. When the *Bengal*'s smoke cleared some twenty minutes later, neither raider was in sight, and the *Ondina* was hull-down on the horizon, heading south. Wilson was satisfied that his commitment to the tanker had been fully discharged.

Unfortunately the *Ondina* was not in as favourable a position as Wilson had presumed. She was, in fact, in desperate straits, for the *Aikoku Maru*, believing she had sunk the *Bengal*, had gone after the tanker, firing with all guns she could bring to bear. Captain Horsman, down to his last twelve rounds of ammunition and also convinced that the *Bengal* had gone down, dropped smoke floats and rang for emergency full speed on his engines.

The smoke floats failed to hide the fleeing tanker from her

pursuer, and salvoes from the heavy guns of the *Aikoku Maru* were soon straddling her. The *Ondina*'s 4-inch continued to hit back, but it was a contest that could have only one end. The tanker received six direct hits, shells slamming into her forecastle, bridge and after pump-room in quick succession. When the news came from aft that all ammunition had been expended, Horseman was left with only one option, and he took it without hesitation. Sending below for two white bedsheets, he ordered that they be hoisted on the flag halyards. The *Ondina* was offering surrender.

The *Aikoku Maru* ignored the signal and continued firing on her helpless quarry. Horsman now had no alternative but to stop his engines and order his crew to abandon ship. No sooner had he given the last order than a Japanese shell burst on the bridge of the *Ondina*, and he was killed by flying shrapnel.

The remaining fifty-six men of the *Ondina*'s crew, most of them unaware of their captain's death, set about abandoning ship. Although the shells continued to burst all around them, there was no panic, and in less than three minutes all lifeboats and rafts were in the water and pulling away from the ship. Ironically, as the *Ondina*'s men were thus engaged, they witnessed the last of the *Hokoku Maru*, which sank stern first, leaving many men struggling in the water.

What little satisfaction the tanker's men gained from the demise of their erstwhile enemy was soon dissipated by the arrival of the *Aikoku Maru*, which swept down on the *Ondina*, her guns still blazing. At 400 yards the raider fired two torpedoes, which passed under the lifeboats and struck the *Ondina* in way of her after tanks. She immediately took a heavy list to starboard and began to settle by the stern.

For the shocked survivors of the *Ondina* there was worse to come. In a vile demonstration of man's inhumanity to man, the *Aikoku Maru* now closed the lifeboats and opened fire with her machine-guns. Five of the survivors were wounded, two of them seriously, including Chief Engineer Jan Niekerk.

Mercifully the raider's fit of revenge was short-lived, and she suddenly sheered off and steamed back to pick up survivors from the *Hokoku Maru*. The tanker men, who had thrown themselves into the water when the machine-guns opened up, now reboarded their boats and rafts. The wounded were made as comfortable as the circumstances would allow, but for Chief

Engineer Jan Niekerk nothing could be done. He died of his wounds and was returned to the sea, which had been his life and his livelihood.

And still the ordeal was not over. After about half an hour the *Aikoku Maru* came racing back, seemingly intent on finishing off the helpless men. Fortunately this attack did not materialize. The raider swept disdainfully past the boats and, having fired a third torpedo at the *Ondina*, which missed, headed off in a northerly direction and was soon over the horizon.

Questioning glances were now cast at the *Ondina*, which, although listing heavily and down by the stern, was still very much afloat. To the survivors she represented sanctuary in a very lonely ocean. Second Officer Bakker volunteered to take the motor lifeboat back to the ship, to investigate the possibility of saving her. With him went Able Seaman Hammond and Third Engineer Hendrik Leys.

Once aboard the tanker, Leys inspected the engine-room and found the main engine and pumps in working order. Apart from being holed and two of her cargo tanks flooded, the *Ondina* appeared to be seaworthy. Working quickly, Bakker, Hammond and Leys flooded sufficient tanks to bring the ship upright and signalled the others to come aboard.

Shortly after sunset the survivors were all back aboard, with the exception of two Chinese ratings, who were missing and believed killed in the machine-gunning. Chief Officer Martin Rehwinkel took command, his first task being to bury Captain Horsman, who still lay on the bridge where he had fallen during the action. Three hours later, after dealing with a fire discovered to be raging in the forecastle store, the *Ondina* was once more under way. She arrived back in Fremantle seven days later, on 18 November.

When both ships were safe in port – the Bengal having made Colombo, the inevitable inquiries began. Predictably, the actions of the *Bengal* were questioned. In some quarters she was accused of having run away, leaving the *Ondina* to her fate, but there was no hard evidence to back this accusation. The minesweeper had achieved what Lieutenant-Commander Wilson had set out to do, and that was to draw the enemy's fire for as long as possible in order that the tanker might be given a chance to escape.

In retrospect, it seems likely that Wilson did the wise thing in breaking off the action when his ammunition was running low. Had he gone back to the tanker's aid, there was little he could have done, and the *Bengal* would almost certainly have been pounded to pieces by the guns of the *Aikoku Maru*. Such action by the *Bengal* might also have stirred the Japanese into machine-gunning the *Ondina*'s survivors in earnest – perhaps murdering them to a man.

Criticism was also levelled at Captain Horsman for having joined battle with the raiders instead of running away, as he had been ordered to do. But Willem Horsman was no coward and, like any master mariner, he fiercely resented the threat to his ship. His Nelsonian gesture cost him his life, but it did result in the sinking of the *Hokoku Maru* and, in turn, undoubtedly saved the little *Bengal* from destruction.

In a war that witnessed so many acts of courage and sacrifice, the fight put up by the *Bengal* and *Ondina* against the might of the two fast and heavily armed raiders went largely unnoticed. As the guns signal the eleventh hour on Armistice Day down the years, there will be few who will remember those who fought, and even fewer who will weep for those who died, in the Indian Ocean on that November day in 1942.

13   The Replacement

The pavements of Middlesbrough were still wet from an overnight shower when John Dinsmore, signed on as donkeyman in the steamer *Samtampa*, hurried through the dock gates, kitbag over his shoulder. It was Saturday 19 April 1947, the war had been over for two years, and it was a fine morning. Dinsmore was cheerfully looking forward to the short voyage ahead of him. His good humour was somewhat dampened when, having reached the quays, he found that his ship had already sailed. The *Samtampa*'s owners, acutely aware of the lack of profit shown by a ship lying idle in port over a weekend, had packed her off to sea in the early hours. Unwittingly they had done John Dinsmore a priceless service.

By the time Dinsmore was making his way disconsolately back through the dock gates, the *Samtampa* had already cleared the Tees and was in the North Sea, heading south-east for Flamborough Head. On her bridge, Captain H. Neane Sherwell had been informed he was a donkeyman short, but he was not unduly worried. The passage to Newport, Monmouthshire, to which the *Samtampa* was bound in ballast, would occupy only a little more than three days. In such a short time one man in a crew of forty was unlikely to be missed. Below decks, in the engine-room, Chief Engineer W.B. Atkinson was somewhat less pleased at the absence of one of his watchkeepers, but he was not disposed to let such a trifle spoil his day. Atkinson, a Swansea man, was looking forward to a few days in Newport, where the *Samtampa* was to lay up for drydocking and minor repairs. He had plans to spend some time with his family, work and the owners permitting.

When the *Samtampa* passed Flamborough Head, the weather continued fine, with a light wind and light sea, although the visibility had deteriorated. No gale warnings were in operation, but Captain Sherwell, knowing the fickleness of the weather on the British coast, was not fully at ease. His ship, flying light, with only 182 tons of permanent ballast in her empty holds and drawing a mere thirteen feet of water, had almost three-quarters of her slab-sided hull exposed to the elements. In a high wind, as Sherwell had learned from bitter experience, she would be hard to handle. But then, one could hardly expect perfection from a Liberty ship.

At the height of the Battle of the Atlantic, in the winter of 1942, Britain was losing her merchant ships to the U-boats at the rate of sixty a month, faster than they could be replaced by her hard-pressed shipyards. In desperation, she turned to the USA, then a vast and largely unstretched industrial powerhouse. The call was for a tramp-style cargo ship, with a large carrying-capacity and economic fuel-consumption – a hostilities-only replacement ship. The Americans responded with characteristic enthusiasm and soon had eighteen shipyards turning out the new 'Liberty' ship at the rate of nearly two a day.

　The Liberty, based on plans drawn up in a Newcastle-upon-Tyne shipyard as far back as 1879, emerged as an all-welded ship of 7,000 tons gross, 420 feet long and fifty-seven feet in the beam. A triple-expansion steam-engine, driven by oil-fired Scotch boilers, gave her a service speed of eleven knots. However, her deadweight capacity of 10,000 tons allowed for no fine lines, and she was really only a huge, unwieldy barge, vaguely shaped at each end and topped by a single block of accommodation, two masts and a short funnel. For her size, she was grossly underpowered, a failing exacerbated by an insufficiency of ballast tanks. In the light condition, her propeller was not completely submerged and thus lost much of its thrust. This, combined with a large area of hull exposed to the wind, gave her a dangerous tendency to make leeway on a par with the windjammers of another age. A Liberty in ballast was not a ship to be caught with on a lee shore in high winds.

　For all their failings, the Liberty ships more than proved their worth in supplying a beleaguered Britain in the 1940s. It was said that, even if a Liberty survived to bring only one cargo across the Atlantic, she had served her purpose. In the event, more than 2,700 of these replacement ships were built, and many of them were still in service long after the drums of war were stilled. One such was the *Samtampa*.

Built in 1943 by the New England Shipbuilding Corporation of Portland, Maine, the 7,129-ton *Samtampa* was owned by the Ministry of Transport and managed by Houlder Brothers of London, a company long established in the River Plate trade. Having survived the war unscathed, she was about to be handed over to Houlders to replace one of their many wartime losses.

Fog in the North Sea slowed the *Samtampa* down to a crawl, and it was late on the morning of the 21st before she began her passage of the busy Dover Strait. As Captain Sherwell had feared, a rapidly falling barometer indicated that the spell of calm weather was coming to an end. A few hours after clearing the strait, she was butting into the teeth of a rising south-westerly wind and losing speed with every wave she shouldered aside. Further down the Channel, small ships were running for shelter, and the 31,000-ton battleship *Warspite*, under tow to the breaker's yard, was reported in difficulties off the Cornish coast.

At 10.00 on the 23rd, after what must have been a long and arduous struggle to round Land's End, the *Samtampa* was sighted off Hartland Point, on the north coast of Devon, running before a Force 8 south-westerly. She was already thirty-six hours late on her original ETA at Newport and likely to be delayed further still. Warnings of severe weather to come had been issued by the Meteorological Office. In the English Channel, the *Warspite* had broken free of her tugs and had been thrown onto the rocks off Penzance by heavy seas.

During the afternoon the 6,000 British cargo ship *Empire Success*, also inbound in the Bristol Channel, was in radio contact with the *Samtampa*. The Houlders ship reported she was about to heave to off Foreland Point, near Lynmouth. It was apparent that Sherwell had been forced to abandon all thoughts of proceeding up Channel and was preparing to ride out the storm head to wind and sea. The wind was now blowing near-hurricane force from the south-west, and the seas were steep and menacing. The scene was set for one of the worst disasters seen in the Bristol Channel for many years.

Nothing was heard from the *Samtampa* for another two hours, then, at 17.14, the radio officer of the *Empire Success* picked up an anguished cry for help: 'XXX SAMTAMPA RAPIDLY

DRIFTING TOWARDS NASH SHOAL.' The Liberty ship, riding high out of the water and with her propeller threshing air each time her stern lifted on the sea, was being blown bodily towards the Welsh coast to the east of Swansea Bay.

Forty minutes later Burnham Radio, which was monitoring the emergency, heard: 'HAVE BOTH HOOKS DOWN NOW AND HOPE TO KEEP OFF THE SHOAL BUT DOUBTFUL STILL.' The exact position of the *Samtampa* was unknown, but local rescue services, including coastguards at Porthcawl and the Mumbles lifeboat, were immediately alerted. Tugs attempted to leave Swansea harbour to search for the ship but were driven back by heavy seas.

In the clubhouse of Porthcawl's Royal George Golf Club, on the high ground overlooking Sker Point, the club's steward, William Price, was making ready to shut up shop for the day. The gale-force winds and driving rain had long since cleared the greens of even the most dedicated golfers. Price was about to lock up when, through a break in the rain, he was astonished to see a large ship looming close inshore, apparently less than a mile off the beach. At that point Price was joined by the station officer of the Porthcawl coastguard. Both men examined the ship through binoculars, establishing that she was stern-on to the shore, with both anchors down and going ahead on her engines in a desperate effort to avoid being driven onto the rocks at the foot of Sker Point. The coastguard officer, realizing he had found the *Samtampa*, asked William Price for the use of his telephone.

At Mumbles, on the far side of Swansea Bay, Coxswain Gammon took the call and ordered his men into oilskins and lifejackets. Gammon then went outside the boathouse to test the full force of the weather. He was not pleased. In the failing light, the bay was a mass of angry whitecaps. Beyond the headland, the waves would be running high, for the anemometer on the boathouse was showing a wind speed of seventy knots. Gammon rasped at the bristles of his chin and thought back to that black night in 1944 when they had taken off the crew of the Canadian frigate *Cheboque* in similar weather. The war was on then, and two of his crew had been over seventy, yet they had done their job – as they would again tonight, if and when the time came.

What happened on board the *Samtampa* during her last hours will forever remain in the realms of conjecture. Her final messages, received by Burnham Radio, first indicated that her anchors were dragging. Then her starboard anchor carried away, and twelve minutes later her port anchor cable parted. Witnesses on shore said they saw men board one of the ship's lifeboats but were unable to see if the boat was launched. Given the sea running at the time, it is highly unlikely that any boat could have survived, even if it had been launched.

From his vantage-point in the clubhouse, William Price watched horror-stricken as the *Samtampa* was thrown onto the jagged rocks of Sker Point shortly after 19.00. Pounded by huge, thirty-foot waves, she broke her back at once. Her forward section then drifted out to sea about 200 yards before that also broke in two. Within a few minutes of striking, the 423-foot-long ship was in three pieces, and through the rain and flying spume Price could see some of her crew huddled together on the bridge, the waves breaking right over them. Unless rescue came very quickly, they were finished.

The Porthcawl Lifesaving Company now arrived on the scene and set up a breeches buoy apparatus on the beach. A crowd of onlookers gathered around them, willing them on, but all efforts to save the *Samtampa*'s men were doomed from the start.

The wind was blowing straight on shore with such force that those on the beach had great difficulty in keeping their feet. The first rocket fired went to the full extent of its 400-yard line but fell short of the wreck. The *Samtampa* was out of reach. More rockets were fired, but a swiftly rising tide was forcing the crew back up the beach, so that their efforts were increasingly in vain. Soon they were obliged to join the crowd of onlookers, leaning helplessly into the wind, their faces spattered by fuel oil borne on the screaming wind from the ship's ruptured tanks.

Immediately news reached them that the *Samtampa* was dragging her anchors, William Gammon and his crew of seven took the 23-year-old Mumbles lifeboat, *Edward Prince of Wales*, down the slipway and plunged into the foaming maelstrom of Swansea bay. The sixteen-ton boat, sliding from crest to trough, raced twelve miles up-Channel and for more than an hour searched the shore in the vicinity of Porthcawl but failed to find the *Samtampa*. As visibility was down to just over one mile and darkness was fast closing in, this was not altogether surprising. The lifeboat was not equipped with radio, so Gammon had no alternative but to fight his way back to the Mumbles to gain more information on the wreck. At 19.10 the *Edward Prince of Wales* put to sea again, and all contact with her was lost.

When full darkness came, the broken hull of the *Samtampa* could be seen as a ghostly silhouette in the headlights of cars drawn up on the sand dunes backing the beach at Sker Point. All hope for the thirty-nine men on board the ship had been abandoned. Their deaths were accepted as another cruel sacrifice on the altar of the ever-demanding sea, for this is a risk men who earn their living on the great oceans must take.

At first light next morning, the storm-ravaged beach was seen to be thick with oil and scattered with debris from the battered wreck. When the tide receded, bodies began to come ashore. Ironically, the first to be found was that of Chief Engineer Atkinson, who had come home to his native Wales for the last time.

Police and coastguards waded out to the wreck and, when satisfied there was no one alive on board, began the grim task of recovering more bodies. While they were so engaged, word came through that the Mumbles lifeboat was missing. The search was widened, and when the broken shell of the *Edward Prince of Wales* was found half a mile further along the beach, the enormity of the tragedy of the night of 19 April was revealed. Unseen and unheard, William Gammon and his gallant band of volunteers had given their lives in the fight to save the men of the *Samtampa*.

The court of inquiry into the loss of the *Samtampa* confirmed only what had always been a fact for those who sailed in the Liberty ships: in the weather prevailing, the ship had become unmanageable in her light condition. There was much talk of increasing the ballast capacity of these ships, of instituting a 'light loadline', but, with the passage of time, the disaster of Sker Point was soon forgotten and the Liberty ships continued to wage their unequal battle with the elements for many years to come. The oceans and shores of the world are littered with their broken skeletons.

14   No Way Back

The year 1947, which saw the tragic end of the unsophisticated and vulnerable *Samtampa*, also witnessed the birth of a ship of a very different breed. She was the 2,694-ton passenger/car ferry *Princess Victoria*, purpose-built by William Denny of Dumbarton for the Stranraer/Larne service.

Sturdily constructed, powerfully engined and equipped with the latest navigational aids, including radar, the twin-screw motor vessel *Princess Victoria* was one of the first drive-on/drive-off ferries to come into service in European waters. Owned by British Railways, she offered car- and lorry-drivers a revolutionary means of transport between the United Kingdom and Ireland and proved to be immensely popular from the start. The method of loading and unloading was simple, vehicles driving on or off her open main deck via a ramp at her stern. While at sea, this deck was closed off by a portable bulwark in the form of two steel, hinged doors five feet six inches high. There was no attempt at a watertight closure; it was considered that the man-high doors were sufficient to stop any appreciable amount of water being shipped over the stern during the thirty-three-mile passage across the North Channel.

Captain James Ferguson, by nature of his calling, was a man who rarely missed the regular BBC weather forecasts for shipping. On the morning of 31 January 1953, over an early breakfast at his home in Stranraer, he listened with care to the detached voice of the announcer warning of severe weather in the Malin area. The wind was in the north-west, promising a rough passage across the North Channel for the *Princess Victoria* that morning. Steering a south-westerly course for Larne, she would be beam-on to wind and sea throughout.

When Ferguson reached the quayside an hour later, it was

still dark; ragged clouds raced low across the sky, and cold rain
lashed spitefully at his face. It was not an ideal morning to be
venturing to sea, but there was a schedule to keep up.

Had Captain Ferguson been the recipient of the mass of
satellite-generated weather information on offer today, he might
well have hesitated to sail on that foul January morning. The
forecasters had correctly diagnosed a depression centred to the
north-west of Scotland and anticipated the usual winter gales
moving east across the country. But what they had failed to spot
was a small secondary depression forming on the south-eastern
edge of the primary. This secondary was to grow and combine
with the isobars of its parent to produce winds of hurricane
force, and would sweep rapidly across southern Scotland to the
Continent, trailing death and destruction in its wake.

The *Princess Victoria* left her berth in Stranraer at 07.45,
having on board, apart from her crew of forty-nine, only 127
passengers, a few vehicles and forty-four tons of general cargo,
most of which was carried on the car deck. This was a slack time
of the year for both passengers and freight. As the ferry made
her way up the three-mile-long Loch Ryan towards the open
sea, the wind was gusting strongly, but Ferguson still had no
reason to anticipate anything more than an uncomfortable
passage. When, at 08.30, she left the shelter of the land, it was
as though she had steamed straight into the mouth of Hell itself.

Funnelling down the narrow gullet of the North Channel,
which separates Scotland from Northern Ireland, storm-force
winds had already built up thirty-foot seas with angry, foaming
crests. Rain and sleet lashed down and lightning flashed as the
small ferry buried her bows deep and staggered under the
weight of water that came pouring over her raised forecastle.
The cries of startled passengers mingled with the crash of
breaking crockery and the thud of falling furniture.

James Ferguson, bracing himself in the starboard wing of the
bridge, half-blinded by sleet and flying spray, recognized that he
had an urgent decision to make. The choice presented to him
was not wide. Altering course to port to put the *Princess Victoria*
on her south-easterly course for Larne was out of the question.
She would then be beam-on to the mountainous seas and would
roll her bulwarks under, with disastrous consequences for her
passengers and cargo, and perhaps for the ship herself. He must
either carry on or go back, but to heave to with the wind and sea

ahead, to hold her riding the crests and plunging into the troughs – as she was now, could only be a short-term measure. She was too near the land and might end up being tossed onto the steep cliffs of Corsewell Point. The sleet had turned to snow, reducing visibility to a few yards, when Ferguson decided he must return to the shelter of Loch Ryan. He must go back.

There was no time to warn those below – not that it would have mattered. Passengers and crew alike were already hanging on for their dear lives as the ship roller-coastered from crest to trough.

Ferguson waited until she rose on the next on-coming wave and then gave the order for full starboard helm, at the same time slowing down the starboard engine to give more torque. The *Princess Victoria* slid down into the trough, turning as she went with an awkward, corkscrewing movement. By the time next sea bore down on her, she was stern-on.

Any ship running with her stern to a heavy sea is in a potentially dangerous position, in that she is liable to be pooped. If the ship's speed coincides with that of the following sea, the curling overhang of a wave may overtake the ship, smashing down on her unprotected stern, causing considerable damage. The effect of the rudder may be lost, and the ship broaches to with disastrous results. The only way of avoiding such a fate is to slow the ship down, so that she rides the backs of the waves like a huge, powered surfboard. It was this action Ferguson took, and for fifteen minutes or more the *Princess Victoria* rode purposefully before the might of the storm, heading back for the shelter of Loch Ryan. It seemed that she would succeed, then she faltered in her step, and her stern slewed suddenly to port. The next wave caught her on her starboard quarter with a blow that shook her from stern to stem.

It was not until the ship began to list to starboard that Ferguson realized something was wrong. Then a report came from aft that the flimsy stern doors had been smashed in and that the car deck was flooded. Had there been sufficient large scuppers in the deck to drain the water away quickly, or a longitudinal bulkhead to restrict the free surface, disaster might have been averted. But with her stern wide open to the sea, hundreds of tons of water surged onto the car deck with every wave that struck. Her cargo shifted, the list increased and the *Princess Victoria* began to drift out of control. Frantic efforts were made to close the stern doors, but they were badly buckled and would not move.

Ferguson was forced to turn his ship again and head back out to sea. He now had only one ace up his sleeve: the *Princess Victoria* was fitted with a bow rudder for manoeuvring when entering port. It was just possible that, by going astern on the engines and steering with the bow rudder, the shelter of the loch might be reached. As this rudder was kept locked in the fore and aft position while at sea, it was first necessary to send men onto the forecastle head to withdraw the locking-pin. The ship's carpenter and two seamen volunteered for the job, but the seas were again climbing over the bow, sweeping the forecastle head, and they failed to reach the rudder pin.

The *Princess Victoria* was now moving slowly out to sea, with a 10° list to starboard and a gaping wound in her stern, through which the sea continued to pour. Ferguson instructed Radio Officer David Broadfoot to send out a call for assistance. The time was 09.46. Two hours had passed since the ferry had left her berth in Stranraer.

Rolling heavily and, through the great weight of water swirling around her car deck, more and more reluctant to return to the upright each time she heeled, the *Princess Victoria* drifted crabwise across the North Channel battered by hurricane-force winds and pounding seas. By 10.30 she was four miles north-west of Corsewell Point, water had entered the accommodation, and her list had increased to 20°. Ferguson passed the word for lifejackets to be issued to the passengers. In the radio-room, David Broadfoot crouched over his key, keeping the outside world informed of the deteriorating situation.

Noon came, with no let-up in the storm. The crippled ferry had drifted past Corsewell Point and was five miles to the west. The list was now so severe that it was necessary to rig lifelines for the passengers to climb up to the port side of the entrance hall, where they had been ordered to assemble. It was certain they would soon have to abandon ship. Ferguson, for all the horrendous problems assailing him, kept up a flow of reassuring messages over the bridge tannoy. His calming influence was largely responsible for the absence of panic.

In response to Broadfoot's courageous work in the radio-room, help was now on the way. The Portpatrick and

Donaghadee lifeboats had been launched, and the destroyer HMS *Contest* was racing south at full speed from her base on the Clyde. But the weather was worsening. The secondary depression, continuing to feed on the primary, was producing winds of up to 120 mph, and the North Channel had become a seething mass of angry, marching waves. Squalls of sleet and snow were at times reducing visibility to zero. The rescue, if it came, would involve a tremendous battle of man against the elements gone wild.

Two hours later the *Princess Victoria* had drifted to a position she reported as five miles east of the Copeland Islands, just south of the entrance to Belfast Lough. She was still under way but had a 45° list. Ferguson was preparing to abandon ship. Radio Officer Broadfoot remained at his post, the ship's tenuous link with the world on the other side of this ghastly nightmare. The rescue ships were a long time coming.

At 13.54, reluctantly concluding that to delay longer would serve no useful purpose, James Ferguson gave the order to abandon ship. In the terrible conditions prevailing, the ship being almost on her beam ends with the seas washing over her, this was an operation that could easily have turned into a chaotic rout. The starboard lifeboats were almost in the water, some smashed by the seas and all out of reach. On the port side, due to the severe list, it was impossible to swing the boats out. Fortunately the officers and men of the *Princess Victoria* were a well-trained and disciplined team. Mustering the frightened passengers as best they could, they cleared away the port-side boats ready for floating off when the ship went down. Their plan might have worked but, as they were in the act of embarking the passengers, the *Princess Victoria* gave one last, agonized lurch and capsized.

Meanwhile the Portpatrick and Donaghadee lifeboats, HMS *Contest*, the salvage vessel *Salveda* and the coastal tanker *Pass of Drumochter* were battling their way through the storm towards the position passed to them by Broadfoot. Unknown to them and to the radio officer, this position was seriously in error – an understandable mistake taking into account the dreadful conditions prevailing on the ferry. When the rescue ships finally reached the spot five miles east of the Copelands, they found nothing. The *Princess Victoria* had, in fact, foundered five miles to the north and one mile to the east. It was only when the coaster *Orchy*, which had courageously set out from Belfast Lough on hearing of the plight of the ferry, ran into wreckage that the real position of the disaster became known. The other ships came racing in answer to the *Orchy*'s call.

Of the 176 passengers and crew on board the *Princess Victoria* only forty-four were rescued, and most of these survived in the port-side boats which had been prepared for floating when she went down. Captain James Ferguson and all his officers died, David Broadfoot remaining at his post in the radio-room until the sea took him.

It was later established that the *Princess Victoria* went down only five miles from the mouth of Belfast Lough. Had she stayed afloat for another half-hour or so, she would have been in sheltered waters. In the summing-up at the subsequent court of inquiry, the learned judge said: 'If the *Princess Victoria* had been as staunch as the men who manned her, then all would have been well and this disaster averted.'

As the complex depression of 31 January moved across the British Isles, it deepened and intensified, spawning winds of unprecedented fury. A sustained windspeed – not a gust – of 125 mph, the highest on record, was logged in the Orkneys. As bad luck would have it, this was also a time of exceptionally high spring tides, and the combination of wind and sea produced in the North Sea storm tides which inundated hundreds of square miles of low-lying eastern England, the Netherlands and Belgium. The death toll rose to over 500, and many thousands were made homeless.

On 6 March 1987 the cross-Channel car ferry *Herald of Free Enterprise* capsized and sank off Zeebrugge with the loss of 188 lives. In this case, the breach of watertightness was due not to the elements but to an appalling lack of good seamanship, in that the ship went to sea with her bow doors open. The opinion of the courts was that the *Herald of Free Enterprise* would not have capsized if she had been fitted with (a) sufficient scuppers to clear the water quickly from her flooded car deck and (b) a longitudinal bulkhead or breakwater to restrict the free surface of water. It would seem that, thirty-four years on, little had been learned from the loss of the *Princess Victoria*.

15   An Ill Wind

The *Dara* was tired and ageing, one of the 'forgotten fleet' of pilgrim-carriers of the British India Steam Navigation Company. Although registered in London, the 5,030-ton motor vessel had not seen her homeland since she came out of Barclay Curle's Glasgow yard in 1948. For thirteen long years, with her sisters *Daressa*, *Dumrah* and *Dwarka*, she had maintained a weekly service between Bombay and Persian Gulf ports, originally carrying Moslem pilgrims *en route* to Mecca and more latterly Indian clerks, technicians and labourers, who, with the coming of the oil boom, had moved into the Gulf in large numbers to service the oil fields and build the new Arab cities.

For the *Dara*'s nineteen British officers and 113 Indian ratings, the Bombay – Persian Gulf run was a hard slog. Calling at as many as twelve or fifteen ports in a round voyage of ten days, with no passage between ports much over eighteen hours, there was no time to enjoy the pleasures of sailing under blue skies and in calm waters. The *Dara* was certified to carry, in addition to cargo and mails, seventy-eight saloon and 948 'unberthed' passengers. The latter deposited their baggage and rested their heads wherever space could be found: on the open decks, on hatchtops and in alleyways. When she sailed out of Bombay to begin her circuit of the Gulf, the white-painted motor vessel often resembled a crowded Mississippi river-boat. Every available inch of space on board was packed with heaving humanity, and would remain that way throughout the voyage. At each port at which she called, those who disembarked would be immediately replaced with an equal number shouldering battered suitcases and untidy bundles, all prepared to do battle for a favoured spot in the shade. Babies were born on board, the old and the sick died, but nothing was allowed to interrupt the *Dara*'s tight schedule. In a land with few good roads and a dearth of railways, and at a time when mass air travel was still in its infancy, the *Dara* and her sisters provided the main means of communication between the Gulf states.

Chaotic and hard-pressed as the *Dara* might appear at times, she was a well-maintained, tightly run ship, classed 100 A1 at Lloyd's and periodically inspected to ensure she remained so. Her hull was sound, her engines were reliable, and her crew was of the highest standard. In order to cope with any emergency, she was equipped with sixteen steel lifeboats with a total capacity of 921 persons, twenty-eight small rafts capable of supporting another 560, lifejackets for 1,350 and the usual standard of fire-fighting gear required for British passenger ships. Fortunately, in all her thirteen punishing years she had never been called upon to use any of this equipment, except at the regular fire- and boat-drills carried out in accordance with Ministry of Transport regulations.

When the *Dara* left Bombay on 23 March 1961, she was commanded by Captain Charles Elson, whose senior officers were Chief Officer P.E. Jordan and Chief Engineer G.K. Cruickshank. She had the usual large complement of passengers and was scheduled to call at Karachi, Pasni, Muscat, Dubai, Umm Said, Bahrain, Bushire, Kuwait, Mina Al Ahmadi, Khorramshahr and Basrah, then back to Khorramshahr, Kuwait, Bahrain and Dubai, before returning to Bombay on or about 10 April. This was a longer-than-usual round trip and a very gruelling itinerary, but Captain Elson and his crew accepted the task with their habitual good grace.

The voyage progressed well until the *Dara* reached Bahrain on the return leg on 5 April. It was hot and humid when she anchored, with ominous, dark cumulo-nimbus clouds building up to the north. The weather in the southern Gulf at that time of the year is normally placid, with mainly light winds and an almost total absence of rain. It was therefore with some surprise that the *Dara*'s deck crew found themselves called upon to batten down hatches when a storm of frightening proportions broke over the port. Thunder rolled, brilliant forked lightning sizzled all around, rain came down in torrents, and the wind blew in fierce, malevolent squalls. The storm raged all day and was, in the opinion of the locals, the worst in living memory. It was late on the afternoon of the 6th before the *Dara* finished discharging her cargo and, having taken on a number of passengers, sailed for

Dubai, her last port in the Gulf.

When she anchored off Dubai at noon on the 7th, the *Dara* was almost twelve hours behind on her schedule, and Captain Elson was anxious to make up for lost time. Fortunately the weather had by then moderated, and the ship was able to commence discharging her cargo into lighters within a short time of arriving.

In 1961 Dubai was little more than a collection of mud huts surrounding a ruined fort and the sheikh's palace, but big changes were afoot. Oil in large quantities had been discovered offshore, and the ruler was anxious to make good use of his new-found wealth. European construction companies had been brought in, and a great building boom was in progress ashore. The result was that the cargo anchorage was crowded with ships of all nations, the majority carrying cement and building-materials. Anchored very close to the *Dara* – uncomfortably close, in Captain Elson's opinion – was the Panamanian-flag cement-carrier *Zeus*. Elson, aware that the coarse sand of the sea bottom in the anchorage was poor holding-ground, instructed his officers on deck to keep a close eye on the Panamanian.

A sudden darkening of the sky at around 16.00 indicated a rapid deterioration in the weather. Soon a strong onshore wind was blowing, whipping up a rough sea and short swell, both of which were aggravated by the shallow water. Elson feared a repeat of the Bahrain storm and was concerned at the vulnerability of his ship in the crowded anchorage. However, the *Dara* was at the time very near to finishing her cargo, and as all passengers were already on board, Elson was very loath to cause another delay by shifting his anchorage.

The captain's hand was forced a few minutes later, when the heavily laden *Zeus* dragged her anchor and drifted down on the *Dara*. Luckily the Panamanian struck the passenger ship only a glancing blow, bending a few rails on her forecastle head and slightly damaging one of the forward lifeboats. But the warning was enough for Elson.

By this time the weather was turning nasty, with the wind up to Force 7 and the sea very rough. Clearly the *Dara* could not continue to work cargo, and there was now a very real risk that she would drag her anchor and perhaps run ashore. Elson instructed Chief Officer Jordan to cast off the lighters and heave up anchor. There was no opportunity to land the shore personnel still on board, and when the *Dara* hove up her anchor and headed out to sea, she took with her seventy-four stevedores, officials and visitors. All crew members were on board, as were seventy-six saloon and 537 deck passengers, making a total complement of 819.

Elson's plan was to ride out the storm by taking the *Dara* to the north-west into deeper water at slow speed. Experience told him that the bad weather was nothing more than the tail-end of an equinoctial depression spilling over into the Gulf from the Mediterranean, and would subside as quickly as it had arisen.

It was as Elson had assumed. The storm abated quickly during the night, and by 04.00 on the 8th the captain decided that it was safe to return to Dubai to complete cargo and land the shore personnel. The *Dara* was at that time about forty-five miles north-west of the port; by steaming at full speed, she would arrive back at the anchorage by full daylight. Having turned the ship around and steadied her on her new course, Elson handed over to Second Officer Alexander, officer of the watch, and retired to his cabin. It had been a long and stressful day.

Alexander anticipated a quiet watch. The visibility was good, it was a straight run into the anchorage through deep water, and few other ships were in the vicinity. When the *Dara* was about five miles from Dubai, he had instructions to call Captain Elson, who would then take over for the approach. Given fair weather, cargo work would be completed in an hour or so, and having landed the shore personnel, the ship would sail for Bombay; seven hours later she would be out of the Gulf, and there would be time to relax. Thoughts were following a similar train in the *Dara*'s engine-room, where Second Engineer Birrell and Fifth Engineer Durham kept watch over the propulsion machinery. The four-to-eight watch settled down to await the coming of a new day.

At 04.40 Alexander broke off from pacing the wing of the bridge and walked into the wheelhouse. The sun being still more than an hour below the horizon, the darkness was absolute. In the wheelhouse the only light was a dim glow from the compass binnacle, behind which the shadowy figure of the Indian quartermaster eased the spokes of the wheel from time to time as the ship yawed about her course. As a matter of routine,

Alexander checked the compass. Satisfied, he moved away from the binnacle. At that moment the sleeping *Dara* was rocked by a massive explosion. The compass light went out, the quartermaster was thrown to the deck by the wildly kicking wheel, and the alarm bells of the fire-detector set up a strident clamour.

In times of peace, an explosion in a dry cargo ship is a very rare occurrence, and Alexander could not have been blamed if he had panicked. The sudden shock, the darkness and the urgent tone of the bells would have unnerved most men. But the second officer kept a firm grip on himself, groping his way first to the panel of the fire-detector, where he hoped to locate the source of the explosion. He was under the impression that it had taken place in the engine-room, and was attempting to confirm this when the engine coughed and died.

Deep in the bowels of the ship, the force of the explosion blew the circuit-breaker off the main switchboard, thereby plunging the engine-room into darkness. At the same time, the air was filled with particles of asbestos lagging, blown from the pipes of the auxiliary boiler. Dazed and temporarily blinded, Second Engineer Birrell, was of the opinion that there had been an explosion of gases in the crankcase. He stopped the engine to avoid further damage.

Captain Elson, who had been dozing in his armchair, reached the bridge as the engine stopped. He took control of the situation at once, ordering that the oil 'not under command' lights be hoisted and sending Alexander below to ascertain the damage. Elson, quite naturally was also convinced that the explosion must have occurred in the engine space, and this theory seemed to be borne out when Chief Officer Jordon arrived on the bridge at a run. He reported a fire raging in the first-class smoke-room, which was directly over the engine-room. The flames appeared to be coming through the deck from below. Chief Engineer Cruickshank arrived a few minutes later with a similar report. He also informed Elson that the steering-gear was out of action, its hydraulic pipes cut. The *Dara* was dead in the water, without lights or steering and on fire below decks. For a ship carrying a large number of passengers, many of whom were liable to panic, this was a frightening predicament.

By this time the emergency generator had been started up,

providing sufficient light in the engine-room for Birrell and Durham to check around the main engine and auxiliaries. They could find nothing mechanically wrong, and there was certainly no evidence of an explosion's having taken place. It was only when they reached the top platform that they came face to face with the reality of the situation. Clouds of dense black smoke were billowing in from the forward tween decks. From behind the wall of smoke came the crackle of flames and the screams of trapped passengers. Birrell ordered his men out of the engine-room immediately.

Both Elson and Cruickshank were still convinced they had an engine-room fire on their hands, and once the area had been cleared, Elson ordered that the engine space be flooded with inert carbon-dioxide gas. The gas seemed to have no effect, and attention was turned to the fire now raging out of control in the amidships accommodation. Hoses were rigged, but there was no water; the pumps in the engine-room were stopped and out of reach behind the smoke and flames. The emergency fire pump was accessible but could not be started.

With his ship and all on board now in great danger, Elson ordered his radio officer to send out an SOS and then sounded the emergency signal on the alarm bells, repeating this on the ship's whistle. Unfortunately this caused blind panic amongst the passengers, who, frightened and bemused, rushed to the boat deck. The fire followed them, and by the time the order was given to abandon ship, most of the lifeboats on the starboard side were unapproachable due to the flames.

The panic worsened, fighting broke out and the officers and crew, striving desperately to maintain a semblance of order in the chaos, were overwhelmed by the screaming mob of passengers. Three overcrowded lifeboats capsized as they reached the water, while others caught fire before they could be swung out. Of the twenty-eight small liferafts stowed on top of the engineers' house, twenty-three were destroyed by flames before they could be thrown overboard. In the space of half an hour, the *Dara* had been turned into a dreadful holocaust, from which it seemed few would escape.

It was fortunate that, when the explosion tore through the *Dara*, the converted tank landingcraft *Empire Guillemot* was near by and had seen the flames. Her master immediately brought his ship close to the burning *Dara* and sent away his boats to assist.

The Norwegian tanker *Thorsholm* also arrived on the scene, to be followed later by three other vessels. In a brilliant combined operation, these ships rescued 584 persons from the sea and the blazing ship.

One of the last rescue boats to go back to the *Dara* took with it Second Officer Alexander and Cadet Grimwood, who reboarded their ship and saved the lives of fifteen terrified passengers found trapped on the poop deck by the flames. Alexander and Grimwood were later joined by Captain Elson, Chief Officer Jordan, Chief Engineer Cruickshank, Fifth Engineer Durham and five Indian ratings. The emergency fire pump was started, and hoses were brought to bear on the fires, but the pressure of the water was so poor that the hoses had little effect. When the *Dara*'s oil tanks went up in flames, Elson wisely decided to abandon his ship for the second and last time.

That evening the Royal Navy frigates *Loch Alvie*, *Loch Ruthven*, and *Loch Fyne* arrived and took over the fire-fighting. But even with all the trained men and equipment at their disposal, the Navy ships had little success. The *Dara* burned on throughout that night, but she was still afloat next morning. The salvage vessel *Ocean Salvor* then took her in tow, with the object of beaching her, but the *Dara*, her upperworks a blackened shell, her engine-room and holds partly flooded, capsized and sank before she reached shallow water.

When the roll was called, it was found that 193 passengers, twenty-one visitors and stevedores and twenty-four crew members had lost their lives when disaster struck the *Dara* early on that April morning in 1961. The cause of the explosion that set her ablaze remained a mystery until divers examined the wreck some months later. They found that the explosion had occurred not in the engine-room, as suspected, but on the upper deck, in or near the first-class accommodation. Further investigations were made and Navy experts concluded that the *Dara* had been sabotaged by persons unknown, using a powerful bomb similar in effect to an anti-tank mine.

It may never be known why the *Dara* became the victim of a saboteur's bomb, for there was no apparent motive for the attack. However, at the time she was lost the first signs of religious and political unrest were beginning to emerge in the Gulf. In Oman and Saudi Arabia, Moslem fundamentalists had embarked on their struggle to take control of a land suddenly become rich beyond the wildest dreams of all Arabs by the discovery of huge reserves of oil. Shootings and bombings had become commonplace ashore, and it is suspected, though it has never been proved, that a time-bomb was planted on the *Dara* during the unprecedented rain-storm at Bahrain. How and why are still matters for debate. But one thing is certain: if the *Dara*'s cargo operations had not been interrupted by the second storm off Dubai, she would have been outside the Gulf when she blew up. In deep, shark-infested waters and with no help near at hand, the death toll in the tragedy would probably have been doubled.

16   Death at the Varne

In the second century AD the Romans built the first two lighthouses in Western Europe, one at Boulogne and the other on the cliffs overlooking Dover. The far-sighted Mediterranean empire-builders realized, even then, that the Dover Strait, western gateway to Europe, was destined to become a navigational headache of the first magnitude.

Today the Dover Strait is the busiest through-waterway in the world. It also remains one of the most hazardous: a fifty-mile-long mariner's nightmare beset by shoals, strong tidal streams and a weather pattern often alternating only between gale-force winds and calms with dense fog. In any twenty-four hours, more than 300 deep-sea vessels pass through the strait, while ferries criss-cross its narrowest part at the rate of one every few minutes.

The rebuilding of the shattered economies of Europe after World War II brought about an unprecedented boom in shipping. Traffic through the Dover Strait doubled and then trebled. Inevitably, as in any boom situation, the sharks moved in. Substandard ships began to appear on the scene in large numbers, predominately under flags of convenience and manned by men to whom the delicate art of navigation was a closed book.

By the 1960s, more than 700 ships a day were flowing through the narrow bottleneck off Dover, and a state of chaos reigned. It was every man for himself, with ships jostling for the right of way, at the same time zigzagging suicidally through the hordes of ferries, fishing-fleets and, in the season, the wandering yachts of the newly affluent weekend sailors of Europe. Major collisions, resulting in the loss of ships and men and in the pollution of the Channel on a massive scale, were taking place at the rate of one a month.

In 1967, in a desperate attempt to bring order out of the chaos, a system of 'one-way' traffic was introduced in the Dover Strait. All ships were instructed to keep to the right, those bound up Channel hugging the French coast, south-bound ships keeping to the British side, passing close to Dover, Folkestone and Beachy Head. Down the middle of the Strait ran an imaginary 'central reservation', not to be crossed except in specific circumstances. The scheme, which envisaged orderly lines of ships proceeding safely up and down the strait in their respective 'lanes', was excellent in conception. Unfortunately it was not legally enforceable, and while the dedicated professional seamen adhered to the rules, there were many who, through either ignorance or sheer bloody-mindedness, persisted in going their own haphazard way. The confusion grew worse, and the number of collisions actually increased. Another four years of anarchy were to pass before the Dover Strait was finally and cruelly shocked into sensibility.

At 03.00 on 11 January 1971, the tanker *Texaco Caribbean* was approaching the South Goodwin lightship, bound down Channel and heading for the sunnier climes of Trinidad, some 4,000 miles to the south-west. On this cold, murky night, as the tanker moved towards the narrows of the Dover Strait, those on watch on her bridge might have been excused if they were more than a little preoccupied with thoughts that included the delights of the warm, tropical sun yet to come.

The *Texaco Caribbean*, a tanker of 20,500 tons deadweight, was American-owned, sailed under the flag of Panama and was crewed by Italians – a typical maritime mongrel. She was an average-sized tanker for her day, the 200,000 tonners spawned by the machinations of OPEC having not yet arrived on the scene. In construction she was of the old, traditional build, with her bridge amidships, beneath which was accommodation for her master and deck officers. Her engineers and ratings lived right aft, over the engine-room. This old-style segregation of the classes on board ship was to soon to prove costly for some.

For Captain Franco Giurini, master of the *Texaco Caribbean*, it had been a long, gut-twisting night, during which he had carefully nursed his ship through some of the most difficult waters in the world. And his ordeal was far from over. Ahead lay the supreme test of a shipmaster's ability, the notorious Dover Strait.

The picture on the *Texaco Caribbean*'s radar screen was a daunting one. Like confetti scattered over the dark void between the clearly etched outlines of the British and French coasts were the tiny, glowing echoes of scores of ships. The smaller echoes, slow-moving and bunched together in clusters, Giurini recognized as fishermen sweeping the rich waters off the Varne and Le Colbart shoals, which for some fifteen miles provide a natural divide between British and French waters. On each side of this divide, a procession of larger echoes indicated the commercial traffic of the Channel, the general cargo ships, the bulk carriers and the tankers. All were, as far as Giurini could ascertain, keeping to their allotted lanes, those bound for the North Sea ports and beyond tucked into the French coast, and the southbound ships, like his own, passing between the shoals and the coast of Kent. At regular intervals small, fast-moving echoes traced their way across the radar screen at right angles to the main streams of traffic. These were the ferries linking Ostend, Dunkirk, Calais and Boulogne with the ports of Dover and Folkestone.

It appeared that all was well, the mariners of the Dover Strait on their best behaviour. Yet Giurini knew that hidden in this tranquil scene might be a number of 'rogue' ships – those who ignored the recommended routes and chose to force their way through the strait against the flow of traffic, thereby endangering everyone. The most frequent violations of the rules took place on the British side, between the South Goodwin and Dungeness, the area the *Texaco Caribbean* was about to enter.

Another matter weighed heavily on Captain Giurini's mind on that January night. Less than twelve hours before, the *Texaco Caribbean* had completed discharging a cargo of petrol and petro-chemicals at the Dutch port of Terneuzen. She was now in ballast, with her cargo tanks one-third full of sea-water and two-thirds full of a lethal mixture of hydrocarbon gas and air. Modern technology has produced an inert gas system capable of stabilizing dirty oil tanks, but the Panamanian did not have the benefit of such an arrangement. She was therefore a floating bomb courting detonation as she made her way down Channel. One spark would suffice to set her off. Franco Giurini prayed for an uneventful passage through the Dover Strait.

At 03.45 the tanker was edging past the Varne lightship, which guards the northern end of the narrow, steep-to shoal

that runs parallel to the coast off Dover harbour. The visibility
had fallen to less than one mile, shutting out the friendly shore
lights and hiding the navigation lights of other ships in the
vicinity. Soon even the red flash of the Varne lightship was
swallowed up in the gloom, and the *Texaco Caribbean* pushed on
in a dark, silent world of her own, with only the regular
heartbeat of her engines betraying her presence.

Six miles to the south-west, unseen by those on the bridge of
the *Texaco Caribbean*, the 9,481-ton Peruvian cargo ship *Paracas*
was also feeling her way through the night. The *Paracas* –
whether by accident or design – appeared to be willing to
sacrifice all the good fortune that had attended her on her
6,000-mile voyage from South America. As a northbound ship,
she should have been on the other side of the Varne Shoal, near
the French coast. Yet she was determinedly threading her way
through the stream of on-coming ships like a single-minded
pedestrian caught on the wrong pavement in the city rush-hour.

Medical opinion has it that in the small hours of the morning,
between 3 a.m. and 5 a.m., the cycle of human life is at its lowest
ebb. Those asleep are said to be as near to death as they ever
will be until their final day comes, while the unfortunate
minority who must be awake are at their most vulnerable. So it
must have been on the bridge of the *Texaco Caribbean* at 04.00
on the 11th as the watches were changing. After four tense
hours, during which he had not once dared to relax his
concentration, it was with some relief that Second Officer Luigi
Fegarotta was handing over the watch to Chief Officer
Giancarlo Ferro. The tired Captain Giurini, conscious that
many more hours would elapse before he could safely leave the
bridge, stood to one side while his officers went through the
handing-over routine. It was then that the *Paracas*, hitherto
unnoticed among the mass of ship echoes on the *Texaco
Caribbean*'s radar screen, was sighted right ahead, bearing down
on the tanker at speed. Giurini had less than one minute to take
avoiding-action.

The time was too short. Even as the *Texaco Caribbean* slowly
answered to Giurini's urgent helm order and began to swing
away from the danger, the great flared bow of the *Paracas* caught
her squarely amidships, just abaft her bridge-house.

Propelled by the unstoppable momentum of ship and cargo,
the sharp stem of the *Paracas* sliced deep into the hull of the

helpless tanker. Steel grated on steel, and showers of sparks cascaded into the ruptured, gas-filled tanks of the *Texaco Caribbean*. The explosion that followed turned the low-hanging clouds blood-red and shattered windows five miles away in the sleeping port of Folkestone.

The shock rolled the *Texaco Caribbean* over on her beam ends, and she split in two, the bow section sinking at once. With it went Captain Giurini and seven of his officers and crew. Those in the stern section were watched over by a more kindly god that night. Several were thrown into the sea by the force of the explosion, but the others were able to launch a lifeboat, and all twenty-two were later picked up by other ships.

The *Paracas*, although her bows were badly mangled, suffered no casualties. She was later towed to Hamburg for repairs.

When daylight came, all that could be seen of the 20,500-ton *Texaco Caribbean* was an oil slick eleven miles long and 300 yards wide, drifting with the tide off the Varne Shoal. Somewhere beneath this grim marker lay the two broken halves of the tanker.

The race was now on to find and mark the wrecks before they claimed another victim from the undiminished stream of ships passing through the area. During the night of the 11th, Trinity House survey vessels traced and buoyed the stern section of the sunken tanker, but all efforts to find the forward part of the *Texaco Caribbean* failed. With this 300-foot-long hazard lurking somewhere close beneath the surface, the southbound passage of the Dover Strait became a game of Russian Roulette that could have only one result. This came sooner rather than later.

On the morning of the 12th, as a pale, wintery sun began its reluctant ascent from the horizon, the German motor vessel *Brandenburg* passed the Varne lightship outward bound, her blunt bows cutting a foaming swathe through the grey waters of the Dover Strait. The 2,695-ton cargo ship, owned by the Hamburg Amerika Line, carried a total crew of thirty-two, including four wives. Her masters and officers were German, her ratings Spanish.

Cautiously the *Brandenburg* skirted the mournfully clanging wreck buoys marking the last resting-place of the stern section of the *Texaco Caribbean* and hurried on down Channel, anxious to be free of this sombre place. A few minutes later she was brought up short and her bottom sliced open over more than half its length. The missing bow section of the Panamanian tanker had been found.

The *Brandenburg* sank so quickly that her crew had no time to launch the boats. Those who were not trapped below were forced to hurl themselves into the sea without even the consolation of a lifejacket. Twenty-one died, including the four women on board. Eleven survivors were brought into Folkestone by some of the same fishing-boats that had taken part in the rescue of the *Texaco Caribbean*'s men only twenty-eight hours before.

Following this second tragedy, a furious row ensued, involving Trinity House, the Department of Trade and various authorative nautical bodies. Accusations and counter-accusations were made and proposals put forward. But no amount of argument could bring back the twenty-nine lives already lost or, seemingly, sort out the worsening traffic chaos in the Dover Strait. For this, the full weight of international law was needed and, as is usual, the nations involved could find little common ground. It was as though there were some who favoured more blood-letting before a full diagnosis could be attempted. They were to have their way.

Meanwhile Trinity House, in a desperate race against time, had four ships out scouring the Dover Strait for the wreckage of its latest casualty. The *Brandenburg* was eventually found lying in twelve fathoms of water close to the two sections of the *Texaco Caribbean*. The area containing the three wrecks was then cordoned off by buoys, supplemented by a wreck-marking vessel. Passage through the southbound lane of the Dover Strait became more difficult, but it was felt that the danger had been safely isolated until salvage work could begin. However, within a few days observers on shore were watching aghast as ship after ship, all with an apparent death-wish, deliberately entered and sailed through the buoyed danger area.

The culmination of this crass stupidity came on the night of 27 February, when the Greek cargo vessel *Niki* paid the ultimate price. Completely ignoring the cordon of green flashing wreck buoys, she steamed at full speed across the sunken wrecks and ripped herself open. The *Niki* went to the bottom in minutes, taking with her all twenty-two of her crew.

Ignorance, apathy and, perhaps, sheer bravado had in the first two months of that winter of 1971 cost the lives of fifty-one men and women in the Dover Strait. Three valuable ships had been lost, beaches polluted and Trinity House saddled with a bill for more than half a million pounds to clear up the mess. But the message had at last been driven home. Twelve months later the Dover Strait traffic separation scheme became mandatory on all ships, and strict policing of the strait was begun by the British and French authorities.

The Dover Strait is now a model of orderly navigation, with only the occasional 'rogue' attempting to re-write the rules. Much of the credit for bringing order out of chaos must go to the maritime authorities on both sides of the Channel and to the dedicated professional seamen of Britain and Continental Europe, who set the example for others to follow. The real impetus for change, however, came from the tragic loss of the fifty-one men and women – innocent parties most of them – of the *Texaco Caribbean*, the *Brandenburg* and the *Niki*. Their sacrifice was not in vain.

17   One for the Record

On an early December morning in 1977, the towlines of Kharg Island's powerful tugs sang in unison as, inch by inch, they dragged a huge, deep-laden VLCC – a 'Very Large Crude Carrier' – from its berth at the Iranian oil terminal. The massive tanker was then slowly canted until her squat bows lined up with the buoyed channel leading out to sea. Her 36,000 horsepower turbines rumbled into life, and the thin pencil of black smoke reaching skywards from her funnel thickened and began to drift astern. High on the bridge of the tanker, Captain Shing-Pao Zia leaned out over the rail and drew a nervous breath as the propeller took a grip on the shallow water, sending clouds of disturbed mud and sand eddying up around the stern. Zia, who was making his first voyage in command of a VLCC, had good reason to feel apprehensive. The 334,030-ton *Venoil*, 1,115 feet long and 176 feet in the beam, was loaded to her maximum draught of 80 feet with 307,045 tons of Iranian crude. Her destination, Point Tupper, Nova Scotia, lay almost 12,000 miles away, on the edge of the Canadian pack-ice.

At her loaded speed of 13½ knots, it would take the *Venoil* almost forty-eight hours to steam the length of the Persian Gulf. By reason of her deep draught (she was drawing over thirteen fathoms of water), this would be a passage fraught with danger. The Gulf, once famous only for its pirates and pearls, is strewn with coral banks, more than one-third of its area having a depth of less than twenty fathoms. In the deep-water channels traffic is heavy, and oil rigs and drilling platforms, many of them uncharted and unlit, abound. Once through the Straits of Hormuz, life would be easier for Captain Zia. The *Venoil* was too big and too heavily loaded to pass through the Suez Canal, and her only route to Nova Scotia lay via the Cape of Good Hope, a long, tedious voyage occupying up to five weeks but, for the most part, in deep water and favourable weather.

The sun which shone down so brilliantly on the *Venoil* as she left the bustle of Kharg Island astern was then only just rising on her sister ship. Far on the other side of the African continent, the 333,935-ton *Venpet* was in mid-Atlantic, returning to Kharg Island in ballast after delivering a cargo to Point Tupper.

With the exception of the slight difference in deadweight tonnage, the two VLCCs were identical in all respects. Built in 1973 at Nagasaki for the Bethlehem Steel Corporation of America, they were, as a matter of economic convenience, registered in Monrovia and flew the Liberian flag. They had been launched at the height of the oil boom, when charter rates were as much as eight times the cost of transportation of oil. As soon as they were ready for sea, they had been taken on a long-term charter by the Gulf Oil Corporation and placed on the Kharg Island – Point Tupper run. Each tanker carried a Taiwanese crew of forty, the masters and officers holding Liberian licences. Navigational equipment in the ships was of the highest standard and included Decca Navigator, which is capable of accurately fixing a ship's position to within fifty yards.

Commanded by Captain Chung-Ming Sun, the *Venpet* had sailed from Point Tupper on the evening of 19 November. There had been no time to clean and gas-free her tanks following the discharge of her last cargo. This operation Captain Sun intended to carry out in the Indian Ocean, where the warmer water would make it easier. Meanwhile the dirty tanks had been filled with an inert gas to combat the threat of explosion posed by the remaining hydrocarbon gases.

It had been planned to make the long voyage to the Persian Gulf without interruption. However, the *Venpet*'s main radio transmitter failed shortly after sailing, forcing Captain Sun to schedule an off-limits call at Cape Town, where a helicopter would be standing by to fly out radio technicians and spares. Sun was fully justified in initiating this action, costly though it might be, for in the world of the oil charter markets, good communications between ship and shore are of paramount importance. A working radio would also be useful to contact and exchange intelligence with the westbound *Venoil*, which Sun expected to meet somewhere off the coast of South Africa.

The *Venpet*'s passage across the South Atlantic passed without incident, and at 10.00 on 15 December a rendezvous was made with the helicopter off Cape Town. Two radio technicians were landed on the tanker and at once set about repairing her faulty transmitter. In order to avoid delay to the passage, it was arranged that these men would be taken off by launch when the *Venpet* passed Durban, some three days later.

Cape Agulhas, the southernmost point of Africa, was rounded at about 16.00, and Captain Sun, with the projected off-limits call at Durban in mind, shaped his course to pass to the north of the Alphard Banks, an extensive area of shoals lying some thirty miles off the coast and forty-five miles east of Agulhas. In doing so, Sun was ignoring a South African recommendation that all ships on the coast 'keep to the right', eastbound ships passing further south than those westbound. After passing the Alphard Banks, the *Venpet* was therefore directly in the path of westbound vessels – and there were many of these in the oil-boom days of the late 1970s. But given that the *Venpet* was equipped with two good radars and that summer at the Cape promised blue skies and clear visibility all the way, Sun did not anticipate any navigational difficulties.

Running south at the height of the balmy north-east monsoon, the *Venoil*'s passage down the Indian Ocean had been pleasant and trouble-free. On a daily basis her radio officer had been attempting to make contact with the *Venpet*, but without success. By the morning of the 16th, the *Venoil* was to the west of Port Elizabeth, and Captain Zia was puzzled by the continued lack of word from the *Venpet*, which by now he expected to be close at hand.

In compliance with South African regulations for loaded tankers, the *Venoil* was steaming at a minimum distance of twelve miles off the coast. The weather was fine, with a clear blue sky and a breeze so light that it barely disturbed the oily calm of an even bluer sea. Visibility was excellent. There was, however, an ominous, damp chill in the morning air. It did not occur to Second Officer Jen-Tsao Yang, who had the watch on the bridge, that a dangerous mix of the elements was at work. Zia, when he came to the bridge, also failed to recognize the warning signs. With a quick look around the empty horizon, he set a course of 267°, which would take the *Venoil* to the north of the Alphard Banks and twelve miles south of Cape Agulhas.

Over the horizon, sixty-seven miles to the west, the *Venpet* was in similarly idyllic weather and steaming at full speed on a course of 084°. Unknown to each other, the two 330,000-ton sisters were lined up on almost directly opposite courses and closing at a combined speed of twenty-seven knots.

Third Officer Burt-Chao Chang took over the bridge of the *Venoil* at 08.00. By then the volatile mixture of low temperature and high humidity had been sufficiently stirred by the gentle breeze, and the once sharp horizon was blurring. Soon the visibility was down to seven miles, and occasional fog patches were rolling in on the deep-laden tanker as she pushed steadily westwards. During the next hour Captain Zia paid several visits to the bridge but ignored the obvious deterioration in visibility. His prime interest lay in calculating an accurate ETA off Cape Town, where, on the following morning, the *Venoil* was to rendezvous with a helicopter bringing mail and fresh provisions – a welcome morale-booster for the crew at the halfway point of the voyage.

At 08.45 Third Officer Chang drew Zia's attention to an echo on the radar screen fine on the *Venoil*'s port bow at twenty-two miles. This appeared to be a large ship approaching from the west on a parallel and opposite course. Twenty minutes later the echo of the other ship was down to thirteen miles, and the bearing on the bow had opened by only 2°. Neither Chang nor Zia thought it necessary at this point to take avoiding action.

On the bridge of the eastbound *Venpet*, Third Officer Jan-Syi Ju had the watch. From the time he had taken over, at 08.00, visibility had been falling steadily and now stood at about seven miles. The radar screen showed the echo of a large ship ahead, and two or three degrees on the *Venpet*'s starboard bow. Ju did not consider that the circumstances warranted calling Captain Sun, who had not yet appeared on the bridge that morning.

At 09.10 the *Venoil* suddenly ran into dense fog, which had been forming in the cold air since shortly before sunrise. Within the space of a few seconds, the long foredeck of the VLCC all but disappeared from sight, and the great ship was sliding through a silent world of opaque whiteness disturbed only by the high-pitched whine of her turbines. A glance at the radar showed Captain Zia that the other vessel was now at 8½ miles, with very little change in the angle on the bow. With a noncommittal shrug of his shoulders, he turned away from the radar and informed Chang that he was going below to consult the radio officer on ship-to-helicopter communications.

Left alone on the bridge, Third Officer Chang studied the radar screen intently and at long last decided that the other ship was shaping to pass dangerously close. After some hesitation, he altered course 5° to starboard, intending to pass port to port.

On the bridge of the *Venpet*, also now in dense fog, Third Officer Ju was likewise at last becoming concerned for the safety of his ship. Unlike Chang, he judged that a starboard-to-starboard passing would be in order and made an alteration of 5° to port. A deadly game of blind man's buff, with two 330,000 tonners participating, had begun.

Over the following twenty minutes, each ship made a number of small alterations of course, the westbound *Venoil* always to starboard and the eastbound *Venpet* always to port. On their respective bridges, Chang and Ju were each convinced that they were altering away from the danger. In fact, the giant tankers, both steaming at full speed and hidden from each other by the fog, were locked into what is known in nautical parlance as a 'culminative turn' – a manoeuvre which could only end in disaster.

At 9.30, with the radar echo of the other ship so close that it was merging with the sea clutter at the centre of the screen, Chang ordered full starboard helm, in a last, desperate attempt to swing the *Venoil* away from the danger he could not yet see. It was too late. The whiteness of the fog ahead slowly darkened and then abruptly parted to reveal a great, slab-sided, rust-streaked hull looming in the path of the *Venoil*'s bows.

The *Venoil* crashed into the starboard side of the *Venpet* and, her protruding bower anchor acting like a sharp-pointed horn, ripped open her sister from amidships to her engine-room. Showers of brilliant sparks shot into the air to fall lazily back onto the thousands of gallons of oil spurting from the ruptured cargo tanks of the *Venoil*. Soon both ships and the sea around them were a mass of leaping flames.

Fortunately for the crews of the Liberian tankers, two British ships, the *Jedforest* and the *Clan Menzies*, were close by. With the aid of a helicopter from a nearby oil rig, all but two of the eighty-two men on board the burning ships were rescued. Those who died, the chief fireman and second cook of the *Venoil*, lost their lives when they jumped into the blazing sea.

Salvage tugs sent out from Cape Town eventually extinguished the fires and took the crippled VLCCs in tow. But little could be done about the 26,000 tons of crude oil that poured into the sea from the *Venoil*'s ruptured tanks. For many weeks after the collision, an oil slick six miles by two miles drifted off the beautiful holiday beaches of South Africa's famed Garden Route coastline, causing pollution on a huge scale.

The *Venoil/Venpet* clash should never have happened. It was a classic example of the misuse of modern technology by those who neither understand it nor have the ability to control it. Even though they had been in sight of each other on radar from twenty-two miles, at no time did either of these sophisticatedly equipped ships make a bold alteration of course away from the other. If only one of them had done so, the disaster would have been avoided. Furthermore, at no time during the forty-five-minute run-up to the collision did the two tankers attempt to contact each other on VHF radio. This they could easily have done and come to an agreement on the avoiding-action each ship would take. In fog, with visibility down to fifty yards, neither vessel reduced speed or sounded fog-signals, thereby ignoring the basic international rules governing the navigation of ships in poor visibility.

It may be argued that Third Officer Chang of the *Venoil* and Third Officer Ju of the *Venpet* were inexperienced junior officers and might be forgiven for a lack of appreciation of the developing situation. But the same cannot be said for Captain Zia and Captain Sun. Both these men, Captain Zia in particular, must have been well aware of the mounting danger to their vessels, yet, for some inexplicable reason, both chose to ignore this danger. When the *Venoil* and *Venpet* finally ran headlong into each other, Captain Zia was drinking tea in the chief officer's cabin, while Captain Sun was ensconced in the chart-room oblivious to the drama being played out in the *Venpet*'s wheelhouse, only a few feet and a bulkhead away from him.

After lengthy and costly repairs, the *Venoil* and *Venpet* returned to service, only to disappear into obscurity when the oil boom self-destructed a few years later. Today they are remembered only by an entry in *The Guinness Book of Records*, in which they are accorded the distinction of having been participants in the world's largest-ever collision.

18 The 76-Million-Gallon Oil Slick

In the eighteenth century the Caribbean island of Tobago, twenty-five miles north of Trinidad, was little more than a pirate's watering-hole, often playing host to the infamous 'Calico' Jack Rackham and Edward 'Blackbeard' Teach. Today its luxury hotels and silver-sand beaches cater for nothing more threatening than clusters of America's sun-seeking tourists. When, in the late afternoon of 20 July 1979, the 210,257-ton supertanker *Aegean Captain* passed off the northern shores of the island, heading eastwards into the Atlantic, it is unlikely that the affluent on their sun-loungers gave her more than a cursory glance. Had they but known the threat this ship was to pose to the island only a few hours later, the tranquillity of their afternoon would have been rudely shattered.

The *Aegean Captain* was loaded to her marks with 200,000 tons of crude oil, shipped at Bonaire in the Caribbean and destined for Singapore, 11,000 miles and two oceans away. Owned by the Quadrant Shipping Company of Monrovia and flying the Liberian flag, the 1066-foot-long tanker carried a mainly Greek crew of thirty-five. On her bridge, as she steamed alongside the palm-fringed beaches of Tobago, was her chief officer, Mr S. Laoudis, and at his side Fourth Officer Piscopianos. The weather was fine, with a fresh easterly breeze carrying away the heat of the day, but on the horizon ahead loomed a line of towering cumulo-nimbus, heavy with rain. The ship's helm was in automatic pilot, and one of her radars was operating on the twelve-mile range.

Thirty miles to the south-east, on the other side of the rain clouds, the 292,666-ton *Atlantic Empress* was heading in to make her landfall off Tobago. Loaded with 307,000 tons of naphthalene from the Persian Gulf, she had just over 2,000 miles to go to her port of discharge, Beaumont, Texas. Owned by the Branco Shipping Company of Monrovia, she carried a crew of forty, including three officers' wives. All were Greek nationals. Her cargo of naphthelene was classed as 'dangerous', having a flashpoint of below 23°C – the flashpoint of an oil being the lowest temperature at which vapour given off by the oil will explode when a flame is applied to it. With the air temperature in the area being close to 32°C, the *Atlantic Empress*'s cargo was therefore in a highly volatile state.

The officer of the watch on the bridge of the *Atlantic Empress* as she approached the land was not, as would be expected in the circumstances, her chief officer. In sole charge of the navigation of this 1,139-foot-long, deep-laden vessel was her 47-year-old radio officer, Zacharis Anagnostiadis, who, while he was said to take an interest in navigation, had no training or qualification in the subject. The ship's helm was in automatic, and one radar was switched on and scanning on the forty-eight-mile range, in which mode it would be extremely difficult to detect ships close by. At frequent intervals Anagnostiadis would leave the bridge to attend to his other duties in the radio-room. During his absences, the ship was left in the hands of the able seaman on bridge lookout.

When the sun went down, shortly after 18.30, the tropical night closed in quickly, and it should have been obvious to those on the bridge of the *Aegean Captain* that visibility would soon be restricted by rain. No other ships were visible on the radar screen, but the rain squalls ahead were showing as a dense white curtain several miles thick, through which the radar pulses could not penetrate. The warning was clear that the tanker was moving towards a potentially dangerous situation. The course of action to be taken in such a case is clearly laid down by the International Collision Regulations, which state: 'Every vessel shall proceed at a safe speed adapted to the prevailing circumstances and conditions of restricted visibility. A power-driven vessel shall have her engines ready for immediate manoeuvre.' The *Aegean Captain* continued to press on at full speed, and Chief Officer Laoudis took no action to warn the engine-room. Nor did he use the anti-clutter controls of the radar to attempt to pierce the approaching wall of rain.

Some fifteen miles away, the *Atlantic Empress* was already in rain – as yet only a fine drizzle, but visibility was falling steadily. Radio Officer Anagnostiadis, like his opposite number on the bridge of the *Aegean Captain*, took no action other than, once more, to leave the ship in the hands of the lookout while he attended to unspecified duties in the radio-room. When Anagnostiadis returned to the bridge, the naphthalene tanker's radar, which remained on the forty-eight mile range, was showing a faint outline of the island of Tobago near the outer edge of the screen. The white clutter at the centre of the screen, caused by the advancing rain squalls, effectively obscured any target which might be within ten miles of the ship. Anagnostiadis made no move to switch to a shorter range, which would have been more revealing.

In the officers' accommodation below the bridge of the *Atlantic Empress*, the scene was reminiscent of a small community ashore settling down for an evening's relaxation after the day's work. Dinner was over, and most of the off-duty officers had retired to the lounge to watch a film. Chief Officer Psilogenis and his wife sat side by side, engrossed in the film. Captain Chatzipetros, uninterested in the Hollywood offering, had found a willing opponent in Second Engineer Laspitis, and the two men were huddled over a backgammon board in the officers' smoke-room. Meanwhile the 292,666-ton *Atlantic Empress*, with her 70-million-gallon lake of highly volatile spirit, moved on through the night at fourteen knots, watched over only by her radio officer/navigator.

At 18.45 Second Engineer Laspitis returned to the engine-room, and Captain Chatzipetros was left without a backgammon opponent. He decided to pay a visit to the bridge. Entering the wheelhouse, he first occupied himself in fixing the vessel's position by radar, using a bearing and distance off Tobago. Having done this, he idly flicked up and down the radar ranges, checking for the presence of other ships. On the three-mile range the screen was completely obscured by rain clutter, and Chatzipetros gave up the quest in disgust. He then left the wheelhouse to join Radio Officer Anagnostiadis, who was standing alone in the starboard wing, the lookout having gone below for a coffee-break.

It was now 19.00 and the rain was thickening, severely restricting visibility. Anagnostiadis had not yet reduced speed, nor had he seen fit to warn the engine-room. Once he had acquainted himself with the situation, Captain Chatzipetros likewise decided that no precautionary action was necessary. The two men stood side by side, chatting amiably and occasionally peering into the blackness of the night.

Three miles away, the *Aegean Captain* was in a blinding rainstorm, with visibility down to less than half a mile. On her bridge, the routine had not changed. The radar screen was completely obscured by rain clutter, but Chief Officer Laoudis had not reduced speed, was not sounding the ship's whistle as required by the Collision Regulations and had not yet called the master to the bridge. The 200,000-tonner ploughed on, unseen and unseeing.

At a few minutes past 19.00, Captain Chatzipetros, still chatting with Anagnostiadis on the bridge of the *Atlantic Empress*, suddenly became aware of the lights of another ship showing dimly through the rain fine on the starboard bow. For a few seconds, Chatzipetros froze, then he hurled himself into the wheelhouse, an anguished prayer on his lips. Quickly he knocked the helm out of automatic and put the wheel hard to port. It was too late. The *Aegean Captain* and the *Atlantic Empress*, totalling between them almost three-quarters of a million tons weight, crashed into each other at a combined speed of twenty-eight knots.

The holocaust that followed enveloped both ships. Oil poured from the ruptured forward tanks of the *Aegean Captain*, and this was immediately ignited by the burning naphthelene spurting from the huge gash in the hull of the *Atlantic Empress*. Soon the giant ships and the sea around them were enveloped in roaring flames. Men cried out in fear, women screamed.

Reaction aboard the *Aegean Captain* was fast. Radio Officer Haralobos, who was at his correct post in the radio-room, rapped out an SOS even as the order was given to abandon ship. A lifeboat and a liferaft were launched on the port side, away from the flames, and the crew were evacuated within a few minutes of the collision. Only one man, the ship's electrician, was lost.

On the *Atlantic Empress*, which now resembled an enormous funeral pyre, chaos reigned. Captain Chatzipetros was trapped on the bridge by the flames but gave the order to abandon ship over the public address system. His crew, with the exception of two engineers who had been killed in the initial explosion, rushed to the boat deck. As no boat-drill had ever been held on board the tanker, the ensuing struggle to launch a lifeboat was doomed from the start. When the boat did hit the water, crowded with thirty-seven people, it began to sink, for the drain plugs had not been replaced before lowering. By the time this was rectified, the boat was half-full of water, adding to the misery of the frightened wretches it held. And their nightmare had only just begun. In the panic to get away, no one had thought to stop the ship's engines, and the forward momentum was such that it was impossible to slip the lifeboat's falls. The waterlogged craft was dragged along by the burning tanker, unable to break free. When the burning oil on the water began to creep up from astern, slowly overtaking the boat, the survivors took to the sea, hoping to swim clear. By the time rescue ships arrived, only fourteen were still alive, the rest having been drowned, burned alive or taken by sharks. Captain Chatzipetros, although badly burned, survived. Zacharis Anagnostiadis perished.

When dawn came next day, the two supertankers were locked together and still burning furiously. They were only seven miles off Tobago and drifting towards the island. Drifting with them was an oil slick fifteen miles long and three miles across, estimated to contain 76.2 million gallons. After a grim fight, salvagemen separated the burning ships, and the fire on the *Aegean Captain* was extinguished. She was towed into port, only to be declared a total loss and written off as scrap. The *Atlantic Empress* burned on for another two weeks, before blowing up and sinking in deep water. To the great relief of those ashore, a benevolent wind steered the oil slick away from the beaches of Tobago, and the island's lucrative tourist industry continued to flourish.

Three thousand miles to the east of Tobago, in a back street in the Liberian port of Monrovia, the brass plates of the Quadrant and Branco shipping companies were quietly removed, for they had both lost their only ship. But the demise of Quadrant and Branco went unnoticed. Monrovia, a run-down, pseudo-American port of 150,000 inhabitants, is home to no fewer than 2,500 separate shipping companies, one for every sixty of its abysmally poor people. Fanciful names, such as All Oceans

Shipping Co, Carnival Carriers Inc., and Golden Fortune Steamship Inc., fill the pages of Monrovia's phone-book, conjuring up an image of the shipping eldorado once enjoyed by the Liverpools of the Western World. But, contrary to expectations, seldom is the heavy chink of gold dollars heard in this land of the freed slaves. Liberia, which has 52 million tons of merchant shipping registered under its flag – nearly six times that under the Red Ensign, is the poorest country in West Africa.

19   The Return of the Pirates

In January 1722, off the coast of West Africa, Bartholomew Roberts, the most successful pirate of all time, died as he had lived, hurling his ship against a vastly superior foe. The death of Roberts, and the subsequent mass hanging of his crew at Cape Coast Castle, signalled the end of organized piracy in African waters – or so it was thought.

Two hundred and fifty-eight years later, on the morning of 17 January 1980, the 275,333-ton supertanker *British Trident* was steaming north, ninety-four miles off the coast of Senegal. At 10.50 her lookout sighted a pall of black smoke low down on the horizon, and the tanker altered course to investigate. An hour later she was in sight of a large Liberian-flag tanker which appeared to be burning fiercely. As the *British Trident* moved in, the other ship lifted her bow and slipped beneath the waves, leaving only two crowded lifeboats in her wake.

Without hesitation, Captain Robert Taylor, master of the *British Trident*, stopped his vessel and sent away a rescue boat. This soon returned with the sunken Liberian's lifeboats in tow and containing the entire crew of twenty-four of the unfortunate ship. It seemed that what might have been another ghastly maritime tragedy had been averted by the timely arrival of the British tanker.

The tale told by the crew of the sunken ship, the 213,928-ton tanker *Salem*, was a harrowing one. Their ship, they claimed, had been on passage from Kuwait to Italy with 193,000 tons of crude oil when, shortly before 04.00 on 16 January, an explosion occurred in the pump-room, which resulted in the engine-room's flooding. The order was given to abandon ship, and all crew members had taken to the lifeboats by 04.30. For the next thirty-two hours they drifted in sight of their ship and watched helplessly as she burned. The end finally came at 09.00 on the

17th, when a violent explosion ripped the bottom out of the *Salem* and she began to sink.

With all the survivors safely on board, Captain Taylor made for Dakar to land them, but he was already having misgivings about his passengers, a mixture of Greeks and Tunisians. When taken on board the *British Trident*, they appeared to be in remarkably good spirits for men who had been through the trauma of abandoning a burning tanker, followed by thirty-two hours adrift in lifeboats, even though the weather was mercifully calm. Furthermore, there was not a smudge of oil or dirt on any of them, and they were dressed in their best 'shore-going' clothes. It was also clear to Taylor that the evacuation of the sinking ship must have been a most leisurely affair, as the survivors seemed to be carrying most of their personal possessions, including large amounts of money and duty-free cigarettes, in suitcases, boxes and briefcases. The lifeboats were also well stocked with food over and above the standard emergency rations – someone had even found time to make sandwiches. As to the ship's papers, all these had been saved, except the vital log-book, which should have described events leading up to the sinking. There were many eyebrows raised on board the *British Trident* as she headed for port.

Then there was the question of the oil slick – or lack of it – left behind by the *Salem* when she sank. Taylor estimated the slick to be three miles long by half a mile across and of very thin consistency. For a ship reputed to have been loaded with 193,000 tons of Kuwaiti crude oil, her sinking had caused very little pollution. This led the British master to wonder why it was that no distress message from the *Salem* had been picked up either by shore stations or by the *British Trident*'s radio officer until the two ships were in sight of each other and only twenty-six minutes before the Liberian ship sank. The *British Trident* carried the most up-to-date VHF, W/T and R/T radio equipment, all of which was manned or monitored on a twenty-four-hour basis, yet the first, and only, SOS had been heard from the *Salem*'s lifeboat transmitter. A chance remark by one of the Liberian's crew confirmed Captain Taylor's growing suspicions: the tanker had left her loading port, 9,000 miles away in the Persian Gulf, thirty-eight days before she sank; It did not require an expert navigator to calculate that the tanker had 'lost' ten or twelve days on her run around the Cape.

A few days later, when questioned by the authorities in Dakar, a Tunisian crew member of the *Salem* claimed that her cargo of crude oil had been unloaded in Durban and that the ship had been deliberately scuttled in deep water to avoid discovery of the loss. This set in motion an investigation that was to last five years and involve in its intricate web so many parties in so many different countries that it was almost impossible to sort out the innocent from the guilty. The *British Trident* had stumbled upon the biggest shipping fraud in history, a fraud motivated by greed which also served dubious political ends.

In 1979, in an attempt to influence the South African government to end apartheid, the United Nations imposed an international oil embargo on that country. The Arab states of the Persian Gulf, from which most of South Africa's oil flowed, readily agreed to adhere strictly to the embargo, and it seemed likely that the South African economy was doomed to grind to a halt within months. But, like all sanctions ever imposed, this was one made to be broken. The South Africans, rich in gold and diamonds, had the money to pay for the oil – well over the odds, if necessary, and they were not about to see their country wrecked by a mere UN directive. The back-street offices of shady oil-brokers in Europe and America began to hum with clandestine activity, and before long the barely interrupted flow of crude oil to the refineries of South Africa had resumed. False declarations, forged cargo manifests and secret sales of oil on the high seas became the popular game of the day. In a seventeen-month period between 1979 and 1981, one Danish tanker company alone supplied a fifth of South Africa's oil needs.

Onto the scene in December 1979 came a 213,928-ton VLCC (Very Large Crude Carrier), owned by the obscure Pimmerton Shipping Company of Monrovia and flying the Liberian flag. She entered the Persian Gulf bearing the name *South Sun*, but before she went alongside her loading berth at Kuwait, her name was changed to *Salem*, while her owners became the equally obscure Oxford Shipping Company of Monrovia. The groundwork had been laid for a gigantic sanctions-busting fraud.

When the powerful Kuwaiti tugs gently eased her alongside the berth at Mina Al Ahmadi, the *Salem*, although owned on paper by Oxford Shipping, was on 'bareboat' charter to a company trading in Zurich under the name Shipomex. The terms of a bareboat charter are that the charterer hires the vessel for a specified period, appoints the master and crew and pays all running expenses. Shipomex was, then, to all intents and purposes, the temporary owner of the *Salem*.

Appointed by Shipomex to command the *Salem* was a 43-year-old Greek, Captain Dimitrious Georgoulis. With him came Chief Officer Andrea Annivas, Chief Engineer Antonios Kalomiropoulos, eleven other Greek officers and ten Tunisian ratings. The *Salem* left Mina Al Ahmadi on 10 December, loaded with 193,132 tons of Kuwaiti crude oil destined, according to the cargo manifest, for Italy. The ship was said to be fully seaworthy, her hull being insured for £10.6 million and her cargo for £24.7 million, all carried on the London market by Lloyd's. She was too deep to go through the Suez Canal, her only possible route to Italy being via the Cape of Good Hope, a distance of 12,000 miles. At some time on the passage southwards through the Indian Ocean, the owners of her cargo, Pontoil of Lausanne, sold the oil to Shell International Trading of London for £25 million. The destination of the cargo was not changed in the course of this quite legal transaction.

Dimitrios Georgoulis and his motley crew of Greeks and Tunisians were a far cry from the swashbuckling Bartholomew Roberts and his men who haunted the Gulf of Guinea 2½ centuries earlier. They carried neither pistol nor sword, nor did they prey on other ships. However, they were playing a variation of the same old game. Twelve days after clearing the Straits of Hormuz, aided by his crew, who had all been promised large bonuses to be paid in Swiss francs, Georgoulis took the ship into the South African port of Durban. Here the *Salem* was secured to a single-point mooring buoy and, in conditions of great secrecy, discharged her cargo of crude into the storage tanks of Sasol, the South African national oil company. On completion of discharge, the *Salem*'s empty cargo tanks were filled with sea-water, so that to any inquisitive eyes she would appear to be still fully loaded when she sailed from Durban.

Quite obviously, Georgoulis could not arrive at his destination in Italy with tanks full of worthless sea-water, so the second part of the devious plan was put into action. The *Salem* proceeded around the Cape and then northwards until she was 120 miles south-west of Dakar, Senegal. In this region, where the regular shipping-lanes pass, the sea bottom plunges to over 2,000 fathoms, more than deep enough for even a ship as large as the *Salem* to sink without trace. Georgoulis was not, however, prepared to put the lives of himself and his crew in jeopardy. When in position, he stopped the *Salem* and waited for another ship to come along. As the masts and funnel of the *British Trident* lifted over the horizon, he set fire to the *Salem*, placed scuttling-charges in her engine-room and took to the boats. Once away from the burning tanker, the portable lifeboat transmitter was used to send out an SOS. It was a plan fraught with a certain amount of danger, but it might well have succeeded, had it not been for the suspicions of Captain Robert Taylor of the *British Trident*.

When Lloyd's the insurers of the *Salem* and her cargo, received word of the deliberate sinking, Scotland Yard's Fraud Squad were called in. Lengthy inquiries followed, which resulted in warrants being issued for the arrest of Frederick Soudan, a Lebanese-born resident of Texas, said to be the owner of Oxford Shipping, Anton Reidel, a Dutch businessman, Johannes Jürgen Locks, a company director of Frankfurt, and Captain Dimitrios Georgoulis. They were charged with conspiracy to defraud the underwriters of the value of the tanker and to defraud the consignees of the oil, Shell International, of the £25 million it paid for the *Salem*'s cargo. Unfortunately, as conspiracy is not normally an extraditable offence, none of these men could be brought to justice in a British court.

It was a stroke of bad luck for Georgoulis and his chief engineer, Antonios Kalomiropoulos, that they were detained in Dakar by the Senegal authorities on a charge of polluting the seas. The Liberian government, fearing that its already tarnished reputation as a flag-of-convenience host might be irrevocably damaged, requested the extradition of the two seamen. Diplomatic strings were pulled, and the men were deported to Liberia in early March to face trial. If proven guilty of fraud, they would have been liable to spend ten years in a Liberian jail, a prospect which appealed to neither of them. The trial went on for some months, then fate intervened again. Liberia suffered a military *coup*, the country was thrown into confusion, and Georgoulis and Kalomiropoulis were set free. During the course of the trial, however, it had been established that Georgoulis had not been qualified to command the *Salem*. He was not in possession of a foreign-going master's certificate, either Greek or Liberian, although he claimed to have commanded small ships in the Mediterranean for some years. He also claimed to have a foreign-going first mate's certificate, but was unable to produce proof of this. Before the trial ended so abruptly, it came to light that the captain had been involved in three other cases of cargo-theft involving considerable sums of money. Dimitrios Georgoulis was an experienced pirate.

The investigation into the loss of the *Salem* and her cargo dragged on and was eventually to involve a host of shadowy figures, six governments and as many police forces. In May 1984 Frederick Soudan was arrested in the United States and in the following year brought to trial. He was convicted and sentenced to thirty-five years in jail. Anton Reidel stood trial in a Dutch court in 1985 but was acquitted on all charges. Johannes Jügen Locks also went free.

In February 1986 Dimitrios Georgoulis was finally brought before a court in Athens and found guilty of cargo-fraud, endangering the lives of his crew and causing a shipwreck. He was gaoled for twelve years. Antonious Kalomiropoulos, who confessed to having been a party to the conspiracy, received a sentence of four years.

As to the unfortunate *Salem*, lying 2,000 fathoms deep in her dishonourable grave off the coast of West Africa, she earned a place in *The Guinness Book of World Records*, being awarded the accolade of 'The Fraud of the Century'.

20　A Bridge Too Far

The morning was bright and sunny when, on 11 July 1980, the 169,044-tonne ore/bulk/oil-carrier *Derbyshire* sailed from Seven Islands, on the St Lawrence River, bound for Kawasaki in Japan. In her cavernous holds she carried a cargo of 157,447 tonnes of iron-ore concentrates; ahead of her lay a voyage of 15,320 miles via the Cape of Good Hope and the Singapore Strait. It was estimated that, steaming at an economical speed of ten knots, the *Derbyshire* would arrive in Japan around 13 September. Many of her crew of forty-one, commanded by Captain Geoffrey Underhill and including two officers' wives, were due for leave on arrival in Japan. For them, the long passage could not pass quickly enough.

Built in 1976 by Swan Hunter and owned by the Bibby Line of Liverpool, the *Derbyshire* was equipped with the most up-to-date navigational aids, including two radars and a satellite navigator. She was powered by a 30,400 horsepower Burmeister & Wain engine of proven reliability and was one of a class of ships designed to fulfil a long-felt need of the oil-tanker operators, who were unhappy that their highly specialized and expensive vessels spent a great deal of their time running empty to the oilfields. The oil/bulk/ore-carriers (OBOs, as they became known) were constructed with large, uncluttered holds, flanked on each side by oil cargo tanks. The optimum aim was for the ship to carry oil in her side tanks on one leg of the voyage, and ore in her holds on the return passage, thereby earning freight for every hour spent at sea. Although the ideal balance was not always achieved, the OBOs did offer their owners a much greater flexibility in their choice of cargoes.

Twenty-seven days after leaving Seven Islands, the *Derbyshire* passed Cape Town, where she received fresh provisions and crew mail by helicopter. Once around the Cape of Good Hope, she moved into the Indian Ocean and set course to pass to the north of Sumatra. From that point she would run south-eastwards down the Malacca and Singapore straits, and then into the South China Sea. It was the shallow waters of these straits that would present Captain Underhill with the first major challenge of the voyage, for his huge, unwieldy command was drawing in the region of fifty feet of water. However, his officers were well qualified and experienced and his navigational equipment of the best, so he had few qualms. When Singapore was astern, the only real danger in the offing lay mainly in the South China Sea, where the typhoon season would then be at its height. But here the great size of the ship would be to her advantage. The *Derbyshire* was 964 feet long and 145 feet in the beam, a floating colossus quite capable of standing up to the worst the elements might have to throw at her.

True to form, when the *Derbyshire* was half-way across the South China Sea, Japanese weather stations warned of a tropical depression forming over the Caroline Islands, 1,200 miles east of the Philippines. The depression would present no great hazard in its early days, being similar in intensity to the gales that cross the British Isles in winter, but Underhill was well enough versed in the ways of the East to recognize this seemingly innocent area of low pressure as the precursor of much worse to come. Sucking up energy from the vast area of open water over which it moved, and inflamed by the rising currents of warm air emanating from small islands and coral reefs, the depression would first become a storm and then a typhoon, the Chinese 'Big Wind'. Being much smaller in diameter than an Atlantic depression, a typhoon is that much more violent, often having winds of over a hundred knots near its vortex, accompanied by mountainous seas and torrential rain. The course of a Pacific typhoon is more or less predictable, the eye of the storm usually moving first west-north-west at about ten knots towards the Philippines, then into the South China Sea to strike the Chinese mainland in the region of Hong Kong. Alternatively, the typhoon may recurve before reaching the Philippines and sweep back to the north-east, parallel to the coast of Japan.

When he received news of the embryo typhoon, Captain Underhill consulted his charts and calculated that, at his present speed of ten knots and assuming the storm did not recurve, the

Derbyshire would meet it head-on in restricted waters between Luzon and Taiwan. This was not an inviting prospect. Accordingly Underhill increased speed to 12½ knots to pass ahead of the storm. His action was proved correct when, at 11.00 on 4 September, the Ocean Routes Service advised him that the tropical depression was still moving west-north-west at ten knots and forecast to intensify. At her increased speed, the *Derbyshire* would pass about 200 miles off the eye of the storm when she was to the north of Luzon. This was close enough, but an acceptable risk.

Then the unpredictable happened. 'Typhoon Orchid', as it was named late on the 4th, recurved and began to move north-north-west towards Okinawa. Had Orchid speeded up after recurving, which is usually the case, the *Derbyshire* would have been quite safe moving along in the wake of the storm, adjusting her speed to keep out of range of the strongest winds. What followed is largely a matter of conjecture, but it seems that Orchid kept pace with the *Derbyshire* as she entered the Pacific. The great ship and the typhoon were moving relentlessly towards an unplanned rendezvous.

On the afternoon of the 9th, Underhill reported he was 300 miles south-east of Okinawa, ' ... WITH VESSEL HOVE TO IN VIOLENT STORM, WIND ENE FORCE 11; WAVE HEIGHT 30FT; CONTINUOUS RAIN ...' Three hours later he informed his owners, 'NOW HOVE TO DUE TO SEVERE TROPICAL STORM: ESTIMATED TIME OF ARRIVAL KAWASAKI 14TH HOPEFULLY.' From then on, there was complete silence, but no real anxiety was felt on shore for the ship's safety. She was considered too big to be in serious danger.

It was only when the *Derbyshire* failed to reach Kawasaki on the 14th, and an impatient consignee demanded to know the whereabouts of his cargo, that suspicions were aroused. Attempts were made to contact the ship by radio, but there was no reply. At daylight on the 15th the Japanese Maritime Safety agency organized an air and sea search along the ore-carrier's planned course and in the area in which she had last been reported. Orchid had by then swept across Honshu and into the Sea of Japan, but the heavy seas she left in her wake hampered the search. It was not until the 18th that a Japanese aircraft sighted a large oil slick near the *Derbyshire*'s last reported position. There was no wreckage and no sign of lifeboats or survivors. The worst was now accepted, and the thirty relief crew members and four officers' wives, including the wife of Captain Underhill, who had been waiting in Tokyo to join the ship, were quietly flown back to the UK. There would be no glasses raised, no joyous reunions for the *Derbyshire*.

Twenty-four hours passed and a Japanese search vessel reached the oil slick and reported oil welling up from below the surface. Samples of the oil were gathered and later compared with samples of bunker oil taken by the *Derbyshire* when she last refuelled in New York. The results of the tests were not conclusive, but the two oils were similar enough for it to be assumed that they had come from the same source. Another five weeks went by, then a Japanese tanker sighted an empty lifeboat drifting off the Philippines, 700 miles west-south-west of the search area. As the weather was still rough, the waterlogged boat could not be recovered, but the name *Derbyshire* and the port of registry, Liverpool, could be clearly read on the boat's sides. This was the only trace ever found of the 169,044-tonne *Derbyshire*.

It may never be known what catastrophic event overwhelmed the *Derbyshire*, for her crushed remains lie 6,000 fathoms deep in the Pacific, and there is no one left to tell of her last hours. An inquiry held by the Department of Trade in London reached the weighty conclusion that, in the absence of wreckage or survivors, the cause of the loss of the bulk carrier could not be established. On the basis of this finding, the public inquiry called for by the bereaved relatives of the *Derbyshire*'s crew was resisted. The department recommended that research be carried out to establish the cause of the loss, but that was all. The relatives were not satisfied with this pronouncement, and the fight for the truth continued in and out of the courts.

Four years later, on Tuesday 18 November 1986, the Minister of Transport dictated a letter to all interested parties declaring the *Derbyshire* incident finally and irrevocably closed. There was, he stated, no evidence to support holding a public inquiry; the forty-four missing men and women must be allowed to rest quietly in their watery grave. The minister was not to know that, even as he dictated the letter, events in the Atlantic were about to blow his case sky-high.

18 November was a bad day in the North Atlantic. With a deep low centred over Iceland, and a vigorous secondary depression tracking eastwards around the periphery of this low,

winds to the west of Ireland were up to hurricane force, and mountainous seas were running. Caught in this devil's cauldron, the 169,080-tonne ore/bulk/oil-carrier *Kowloon Bridge* found herself running into serious difficulties. Loaded down to her marks with 160,000 tonnes of iron ore from Seven Islands and bound for the Clyde, she had been bucking heavy seas throughout her Atlantic crossing. When, to the south-west of Ireland, the 970-foot-long vessel began to show signs of breaking up, her master, Captain S.T. Rao, decided to run for a port of refuge.

On the morning of the 20th, the Dutch-owned, Hong Kong-flag *Kowloon Bridge*, manned by Indian officers and Turkish ratings (a typical flag-of-convenience mongrel), anchored in Bantry Bay, a deep-water fiord in south-west Ireland. Surveyors who rushed to the scene discovered serious fractures in the deck of the giant bulk carrier immediately forward of her tall bridge structure. This more than justified Captain Rao's decision to seek shelter. It also opened up a can of wriggling worms which had remained tightly closed for four years, for it was revealed that the *Kowloon Bridge* was a sister ship of the *Derbyshire*.

It then came to light that in the winter of 1982 the 169,428-tonne *Tyne Bridge*, another sister of the *Derbyshire*, had been abandoned by her crew in a storm in the North Sea. Fortunately the *Tyne Bridge* did not sink, and after she had been towed into port an examination showed massive cracks in her deck plating, just forward of the bridge, the most vulnerable point in the vessel's hull. She had been very near to breaking in two.

It was now evident that the pedigree of the 'Bridge' class of ore/bulk/oil-carriers required close scrutiny, and to do this it was necessary to go back fifteen years. Between 1971 and 1976 the renowned Swan Hunter yard in Middlesbrough built six OBOs in this class, all supposedly identical. However, it was now discovered that after the completion of the first ship alterations were made in the approved plans with regard to the construction of the watertight bulkhead immediately forward of the bridge. This change was incorporated in the five other ships built, amongst which were the *Tyne Bridge*, the *Kowloon Bridge* and the *Derbyshire* (built as the *Liverpool Bridge*). Continuity of strength was sacrificed in the interests of economy by cutting the fore and aft bulkheads of these ships where they met the athwartships bridge front bulkhead. This created a crucial weakness in the longitudinal strength of the ships. It was also disclosed that a lighter grade of steel had been used in the building of the *Tyne Bridge*, and it seemed highly likely that those who followed after her had suffered a similar economy.

All but one of the 'Bridge' class, it seems, had dangerous weaknesses and, from the evidence gathered, it be argued that the *Derbyshire* was not strong enough to withstand Typhoon Orchid. The continuous flexing of her 970-foot-long hull in the huge swells had caused her to break in two at her weakest point, which, due to the cutting of the longitudinal bulkheads, was just forward of the bridge. The stern part of the ship, which housed the heavy propulsion machinery and on which the bridge and accommodation blocks stood, would have gone to the bottom in seconds, thereby accounting for the lack of any distress message.

The *Kowloon Bridge*, it appeared, had been narrowly saved from a similar fate by the decision of her master to take shelter in Bantry Bay. Unfortunately the story did not end there. Bantry Bay lies open to the south-west, and when the wind shifted into that quarter, as it inevitably does, the anchored ore-carrier was once again in danger. At 08.00 on 22 November, three days after her arrival, the *Kowloon Bridge* snapped her anchor cable. Captain Rao deemed it wise to put to sea again, rather than risk colliding with other ships sheltering in the bay.

It was with some difficulty that Rao took the *Kowloon Bridge* out of Bantry Bay, but his real troubles began when he reached the open sea, where the storm that had forced him to take refuge was still blowing unabated. At 14.23 Rao reported he was off Mizen Head, was battling against Force 10 winds and had already lost one of his inflatable liferafts overboard. Nine hours later the *Kowloon Bridge*'s rudder carried away and, unable to steer, she was completely at the mercy of the great seas running in from the Atlantic. In response to her 'Mayday' call, two RAF helicopters scrambled, and at 01.20 on the 23rd Rao and his crew of twenty-seven were plucked to safety. The Sea King crews who risked their lives to bring off the rescue reported 75 mph winds, with the rudderless ore-carrier rolling wildly in a mountainous eighty-foot swell.

Left to her own devices and – such had been the panic to leave her – with her engines still running, the *Kowloon Bridge* sailed on through the fury of the storm for another twenty hours before finally running onto the Stags Rocks, near Baltimore on the wild coast of County Cork. She remains there to this day, a poignant reminder of the men and women of the *Derbyshire*, for whom there had been no rescue.

21   A Lamb to the Slaughter

The delicate cherry blossoms of Kyushu were in full bloom when, on 24 April 1981, the 10,242-ton bulk carrier *Pacific Charger* first wetted her keel in the blue waters of the ocean for which she was named. Built by Sasebo Heavy Industries, she had been constructed and equipped to the highest specifications of the Nippon Kaiji Kyokai, Japan's equivalent of Lloyd's Register. Her powerful diesel engines, which gave her a speed of 15½ knots, ran sweetly and her paintwork shone. The *Pacific Charger* was a ship full of pride but destined to be dragged down into the very depths of ignominy by the complicated web of financial intrigue in which she found herself caught.

Delivered to the order of Ocean Chargers Ltd of Monrovia, a 'brass plate' subsidiary of the Kansai Shipping Company, the *Pacific Charger*, although Japanese-built and owned, took to the water under the flag of convenience of Liberia. Within days of her delivery, Ocean Chargers chartered her back to Kansai Shipping, who in turn contracted her to Crusader-Swire of Hong Kong to be engaged in their regular service between Japan and New Zealand. Further to cloud an already blurred situation, Kansai then appointed the Harmony Maritime Company of Taiwan to manage the ship. Harmony Maritime handed over the recruitment of the ship's crew to the Union Maritime Company of Taiwan and the Ocean Services Company of Hong Kong. The former was asked to supply Taiwanese officers and the latter Burmese ratings. By the time she sailed from Sasebo, no fewer than six different companies and five nations were involved in the destiny of the *Pacific Charger*.

Appointed to command the *Pacific Charger* on her maiden voyage was 57-year-old Captain Chiou Ruey Yang. Chinese-born Chiou had spent twenty-two years in fishing-vessels and small coastal ships before being awarded, without examination, a Taiwanese ocean-going master's licence. On the strength of this licence, plus the payment of $20 US, he subsequently obtained a Liberian master's certificate and was therefore, in the eyes of the international marine community, qualified to command any deep-sea ship under the Liberian flag. He had no radar training, and his knowledge of English, *lingua franca* of the sea, was extremely limited.

In comparison, the master of a British ocean-going merchant ship must hold a British foreign-going master's certificate, which he may gain only after serving at least 7½ years at sea. The examinations for this certificate, which cover all aspects of navigation, seamanship and ship-management, last a gruelling five days, and a 70 per cent pass-mark is required. Particular attention is paid to the operation and application of radar and other electronic navigational aids. It is normal that, after obtaining his master's certificate, a man will serve another ten or twelve years as watch-keeping officer, finally gaining his command, if he is judged suitable, with at least twenty years experience of deep-sea sailing behind him.

Captain Chiou's deputy in the *Pacific Charger* was First Mate Chang Yung Chung, aged forty-three, who had previously sailed as first mate in Liberian and Panamanian ships. He held a Liberian first mate's certificate issued on the strength of a Taiwanese third mate's licence. The ship's navigator was Second Mate Kao Hing Ho, aged fifty-one, an ex-boatswain. Kao had a Liberian second mate's certificate for which he had paid $40 US. Completing the *Pacific Charger's* complement of deck officers was a 24-year-old third mate who had spent only eighteen months at sea and held a Taiwanese coastal third mate's licence. Like Captain Chiou, none of these officers had had any formal radar training.

In charge of the ship's engine-room was a 54-year-old chief engineer who had served as a petty officer in the Chinese Navy. He claimed to hold a Taiwanese chief engineer's licence. His first assistant engineer held a Liberian certificate issued a few days before he joined the ship, supposedly on the production of a Taiwanese engineer's licence. The second assistant engineer had thirty years experience at sea as an engine-room rating. He had passed no examination but had been able to obtain a Liberian first engineer's certificate shortly before joining. Of the ship's third assistant engineer little is known, other than that he had no paper qualifications.

The *Pacific Charger*'s Burmese ratings appear to have been of indifferent ability. However, if they had been well officered, this would have been of little consequence. It later came to light that these seamen, although signed on articles at International Transport Federation rates of pay, had also signed a second set of articles agreeing to accept substantially less money. This could well have accounted for a certain lack of motivation amongst these men.

This was the state of the *Pacific Charger* when she completed loading at Yokohama and set off on her 5,000-mile voyage to New Zealand. She was a new ship, well found, correctly loaded and seaworthy in all respects, except one – the competency of her master and crew was seriously in doubt.

Wellington, capital city of New Zealand, lies at the south-western end of the North Island. It has a fine natural harbour, whose entrance is unfortunately open to the turbulent winds that plague the Cook Strait all year round. In the early hours of the morning of 21 May 1981, a vigorous south-south-easter was roaring through the heads, kicking up angry white horses on the waters of the outer harbour.

Peering out of the rain-swept windows of the signal station on Beacon Hill, the duty pilot, Captain Smith, cursed the ship that had chosen such a morning to arrive. He had no details of the *Pacific Charger*, other than that she flew a Liberian flag and had come from Japan via Auckland, but he was of the firm opinion that her master would be well advised to wait for daylight before approaching the port. The entrance to the harbour, between Pencarrow Head and Barrett's Reef, is no more than 1½ miles wide and swept by strong tidal streams; no place for a stranger to be testing his mettle on a dark, stormy night. However, the *Pacific Charger* had requested a pilot for 03.00, and Smith would be obliged to make every effort to bring her in.

Shortly after 01.00 the *Pacific Charger* was south of Cape Palliser, at the eastern end of Cook Strait, with thirty miles to go to the Wellington pilot station off Pencarrow Head. It was a black night, lashed by rain squalls borne on a gale-force south-south-easterly wind. A rough sea and heavy swell racing in on the port quarter gave the ship an uncomfortable, dipping, rolling motion. On the bridge, Second Mate Kao had been joined by Captain Chiou. Neither man was familiar with the Cook Strait, and they viewed the task ahead with some apprehension. On such a foul night it would not be easy to find, let alone enter, Wellington harbour. Now would have been the time to turn around, to steam back out to sea to await daylight or a moderation in the weather. Unfortunately Chiou, although he had been in command for a number of years, did not fully appreciate the difficulties facing him. He elected to carry on, navigating on a small-scale ocean chart and with only a vague idea in his head of the intricacies of the entrance to the outer harbour of Wellington. He did not see fit to make use of the large-scale charts of the Cook Strait or to consult the Admiralty Pilot book, both of which were on board.

At 02.00 the *Pacific Charger* was ten miles off the Wellington pilot station and pressing on in a strengthening wind and falling visibility. Captain Chiou was hunched over the radar while Second Mate Kao, having abandoned all pretence at being the ship's navigator, was keeping a lonely lookout in the wing of the bridge. At the wheel was Quartermaster Soe Tint, who had no experience of steering the ship in restricted waters. There was still time to abort the approach, but Chiou was not of that mind. Unclipping the handset of the VHF, he called Beacon Hill and confirmed his ETA as 03.00.

By this time the Wellington pilot, Captain Smith, was already aboard his launch and outward bound for the pilot station off Pencarrow Head. Conditions in the outer harbour were bad, the small but powerful pilot launch having great difficulty in making headway against the wind and sea. Smith called the ferry *Aramoana*, which he knew to be in the Cook Strait, and learned from her that storm-force winds were blowing in the strait. It was clear to Smith that it would be too rough to board the *Pacific Charger* outside the heads. He contacted Chiou on VHF and voiced his fears, hoping that the captain would agree to stand off, at least until daylight. In his broken English Chiou replied that he intended to enter the harbour on arrival and would follow the pilot launch in if Smith could not board. Under the circumstances, Smith considered this was perhaps the best compromise he could achieve.

To the south-east of Pencarrow Head conditions were even worse than the *Aramoana* had reported. The wind was hurricane force, gusting to seventy knots, and the air was full of flying spray torn from the crests of the angry waves which marched the length of the strait under a low canopy of racing clouds. Rain and spray had reduced visibility to 1½ miles. On the bridge of the *Pacific Charger*, Captain Chiou, alternating between radar and chart and at the same time attempting to keep contact with the pilot launch on VHF, was rapidly losing control of the situation. In the dim light of the compass binnacle, fear showed on the face of Quartermaster Soe Tint as he fought inexpertly to keep the ship on course. The *Pacific Charger* was sheering wildly under the influence of the great seas thundering in on the quarter. Second Mate Kao, crouched in the wing of the bridge, was taking no part in the one-sided battle.

At 02.46 Chiou's hastily plotted radar bearings put the ship close to the south-west of Baring Head and apparently clear to enter Wellington harbour. He reduced speed and ordered Soe Tint to steer due north.

A few minutes later the pilot launch clawed her way around Pencarrow Head, and Smith picked up the *Pacific Charger* on his radar. The Liberian ship was less than a mile off Baring Head and making straight for the shore. Horrified, Smith snatched up the VHF handset and screamed a warning over the air to Chiou. It was too late. The 10,242-ton *Pacific Charger* ended her maiden voyage by driving hard on the jagged rocks at the foot of Baring Head.

Thanks mainly to the magnificent efforts of the New Zealand rescue services, there were no human casualties in the *Pacific Charger*'s grounding. The ship herself, although suffering grievous bottom damage, was refloated sixteen days later and towed into Wellington.

There can be no doubt that the stranding of the *Pacific Charger* was due to the bad navigation and seamanship of her Master, aided by the complete incompetence of the so-called navigator. In view of the weather prevailing at the time, Chiou should not have entered the Cook Strait on that terrible night. His subsequent attempt to enter Wellington harbour, using a small-scale chart and without having fully studied the hazards involved, was sheer folly.

Concerning the Liberian certificates of competency which enabled Chiou and his officers to take this unfortunate ship on her maiden voyage, it must be said that they were obtained under the most dubious circumstances. They were, in fact, little more than scraps of worthless paper.

When the dust of the courts of inquiry had finally settled, Second Mate Kao Hing Ho, who admitted that his Liberian certificate was fraudulent, gave up his sea-going career and retired to live a less dangerous life on shore in Taiwan. Captain Chiou Ruey Yang merely changed flag. He was last heard of in command of the 28,776-ton Panamanian bulk carrier *Orient Treasury* as she passed through the Suez Canal, bound for Sweden with 27,000 tons of chrome ore, in February 1982. A few days later she disappeared without trace. Piracy is suspected.

22   Programmed to Disaster

On 17 January 1983 the 138,823-tonne Liberian-registered
tanker *Tifoso*, owned by the Clockwork Corporation of
Monrovia, sailed from Boston, Massachusetts, and headed out
into a stormy Atlantic. She was bound for Port Gentil in West
Africa.

Once clear of Cape Cod and the Nantucket Shoals, Captain
Kyriakis Dimitriadis set course for the Cape Verde Islands,
where the *Tifoso* would replenish her bunkers. The distance to
go was some 2,800 miles, a passage which she would be
expected to complete in eight days.

The weather in the open Atlantic was typical for the winter
months, with a long, threatening swell, a rough sea and an
unending procession of vicious rain squalls racing in under grey
skies. The huge tanker, in ballast and riding high out of the
water, was little affected by the Atlantic's ill humour. Even if she
had been, it is likely there would have been few complaints from
her crew. Only a few days earlier the *Tifoso* had been in her
ninth month of unemployment, seemingly condemned to spend
her declining years gathering weed and rust on the Boston
waterfront. At that time she was just another pathetic casualty
resulting from a sudden world glut of oil and the subsequent
massive surplus of tanker tonnage. More than 340 of her
ungainly sisters, totalling 62 million tonnes deadweight, were
similarly rotting away in the creeks and backwaters of the world.

In early January 1983 the *Tifoso* had been born again. Out of
the blue came a charter for her to carry 100,000 tonnes of crude
oil from Port Gentil, in the Gabon, to Taiwan, and preparations
were soon in hand to bring the tanker out of her enforced
retirement. A survey was carried out by the American Bureau of
Shipping, and the *Tifoso* was declared seaworthy in all respects
for the projected voyage. Her 71-year-old master, Captain

Georgios Giannoules, was replaced by a younger man, 45-year-old Captain Kyriakis Dimitriadis, but the elderly Giannoules was not 'thrown on the beach': when the *Tifoso* left Boston, he sailed in her as second officer.

The first in what was to be a series of unexplained disasters struck the Liberian ship in the early hours of the morning of the 18th. The tanker was well clear of the American coast and settled on her south-easterly course for the Cape Verdes, pushing through the darkness at a comfortable and economical speed. Without warning, the 750kW generator providing electrical power for the ship ground to a sudden halt. The regular thump of the *Tifoso*'s engines ceased abruptly, all lights failed and the giant tanker lay wallowing helplessly in the deep Atlantic troughs.

Chief Engineer Valmas, aroused from his sleep by the eerie silence, pulled on a boilersuit and dashed for the engine-room. Reaching the generator flat, he found Third Assistant Engineer Eleftheroglou struggling to restart the big generator. This, Valmas soon discovered, was a hopeless task. The machine, mysteriously starved of lubricating oil, had overheated and seized solid. Fortunately it was a simple operation to start up the *Tifoso*'s second generator, and she was soon under way again.

The next blow, a near carbon-copy of the first, fell almost exactly twenty-four hours later. This time Chief Engineer Valmas reached the engine-room to find Eleftheroglou shrugging his shoulders over the second generator, which had been wrecked by a sudden and inexplicable failure of the stator windings.

Power was once again restored to the helpless *Tifoso* by bringing into use her emergency steam-driven generator. But this machine was not designed to sustain a ship of the *Tifoso*'s size on a long passage. It seemed that Dimitriadis had no choice but to make for the nearest port at which repair facilities were available. This was Hamilton, Bermuda, which lay handy, only 300 miles to the south.

Bermuda, an island some twelve miles by three miles, is ringed by dangerous reefs, with the Great Bermuda Reef in the north extending to nearly seven miles off the coast. To approach from the north, as the *Tifoso* would be obliged to do, is therefore a hazardous operation. It should not, however, have been beyond the capability of an experienced navigator like Dimitriadis.

The tanker had on board no large-scale chart of the approaches to Bermuda, and Dimitriadis is said to have drawn up his own chart on plain paper, plotting the various beacons and buoys guarding the Great Bermuda Reef with the aid of the Admiralty List of Lights, which formed part of the *Tifoso*'s navigational library. There was nothing particularly unusual in this. It has long been a common practice for ship-masters faced with the necessity of making a strange port for which they have no proper chart. However, it can be a dangerous practice for the less than careful navigator. From time to time, whether by *force majeur* or by design, navigational marks are liable to be missing, unlit or off-station. Fortunately weekly 'Notices to Mariners' are issued covering any such changes, and it is to these notices that the navigator drawing up his own chart must pay particular attention. Before sailing from Boston, the *Tifoso* had been supplied with a full set of such notices. There was no reason, therefore, why the chart constructed by Dimitriadis should have been other than completely accurate.

At 04.00 on 20 January, the *Tifoso* was sixteen miles to the north of Bermuda, which could then be seen as a diffused glow of light on the otherwise dark horizon. The weather was not good, with the wind gusting to gale force from the north-west and kicking up a rough sea. At times visibility was reduced by heavy rain squalls. Captain Dimitriadis was on the bridge, with ex-Captain Giannoules as officer of the watch.

Plotted on the tanker's home-made chart were three light beacons marking the northern edge of the Great Bermuda Reef and the North-east Breaker buoy, moored close to the north-eastern extremity of the reef. The lights on the beacons were said by the Admiralty List of Lights to have a range of twelve miles in clear weather. One of the beacons, the North-east Breaker, was fitted with a radar responder, a device which positively identifies a navigational mark on a ship's radar screen. Dimitriadis's plan is said to have been to sight the North-east Breaker buoy and then shape course to pass to the east of the reef, and thence to a position off St David's lighthouse, where he hoped to pick up a pilot to guide him into the port of Hamilton.

At 04.08 Dimitriadis had on his radar screen what he later referred to as 'a broken image' of the island. There had been, as yet, no visual sighting of the flashing beacons, which should then

have been about seven miles off. He assumed that they were
temporarily blotted out by rain squalls. The North-east Breaker
buoy, which Dimitriadis was making for, was estimated to be
just under six miles ahead but was unlikely to be seen at that
distance owing to the heavy sea running.

By 04.15, the atmosphere on the bridge of the *Tifoso* was
tense, as the two master mariners and the seaman on lookout
strained their eyes to sight the reassuring flash of the buoy,
which should then have been only three miles off and 20° on the
starboard bow. When, at long last, a flashing white light was
seen at 40° on the starboard bow, all three men heaved a great
sigh of relief. The North-east Breaker buoy had been found.

The wide angle on the bow of the buoy must have indicated to
Dimitriadis that the ship was well to the east of her intended
track. To correct this, he ordered a 10° alteration of course to
starboard. At this point, neither the North Rock nor the
North-east Breaker beacon had been sighted, even though the
nearer of these two twelve-mile lights should have been no more
than six miles off. Likewise, the radar responder of the
North-east Breaker had not yet shown up on the radar screen.

At 04.40 the 138,823-tonne *Tifoso* steamed straight onto the
Great Bermuda Reef, ripping her bottom open from stem to
stern.

Had the *Tifoso* grounded on the Great Bermuda Reef, say fifty
years ago, her loss would have been put down to an 'Act of God'
– and with good reason. It was a dark, stormy night, with
uncertain visibility, and she was making her approach to the
island without the benefit of a proper chart. However, the art of
navigation has progressed a long way since the 1930s.

The *Tifoso*, a ship more than ten times the size of her
pre-World War II forbears, was equipped with two radars, a
Loran receiver, a radio direction-finder and an echo-sounder.
All these aids to navigation were to have been in good order
when the ship was surveyed prior to leaving Boston. The Loran,
an extremely accurate system of hyperbolic radio navigation,
would have been capable of fixing the tanker's position to within
a fraction of a mile throughout her passage south from Boston.
Twenty-five miles or so off Bermuda, her radars should have
given a clear picture of the outline of the island, enabling
Dimitriadis to confirm the Loran position beyond doubt. Closer
in, the radar responder on the North-east Breaker beacon

should have been visible on the radar screen, clearly identifying the beacon. In the unlikely event of further proof's being needed, radio direction-finder bearings taken off the Bermuda radio beacon and the depth of water shown by the echo-sounder would have confirmed that the ship was running into danger. Then why did the *Tifoso* pile up on the reef?

At the court of inquiry held following the loss of the *Tifoso*, the incredible conclusion was reached that Captain Dimitriadis had failed to use radar, Loran or any other of his navigational aids to fix the position of his ship when approaching Bermuda. Furthermore, it was stated that the North-east Breaker buoy, which Dimitriadis had supposedly relied upon during his approach, was in fact no longer there. This buoy had been removed as far back as May 1982, and a 'Notice to Mariners' promulgating the change had been put on board the ship at Boston. It would have been the responsibility of Georgios Giannoules, in his temporary capacity of second officer, to bring this notice to the attention of the master. Why had he not done so?

When asked by the court to produce the chart he had drawn up for the approach to Bermuda, Dimitriadis said he had destroyed it soon after the stranding. The ship's log-book was saved, but it contained no record of courses steered directly before the *Tifoso* came to grief. The small-scale ocean chart showed that the initial course steered had been directly for the island.

Fortunately, apart from the ship herself, there were no casualties in the *Tifoso* stranding. The tanker landed on the reef in an upright position and remained that way for some days. Her crew was taken off and 700 tons of bunker oil were transferred to a barge before she was refloated on 2 February and towed out to sea to be scuttled in deep water.

Even to the layman, the grounding of the *Tifoso* must appear mysterious, if not bewildering. For the experienced seaman, it is impossible to comprehend how an apparently well-found tanker, equipped with all modern navigational aids and with two qualified master mariners on her bridge, could have blundered into the Great Bermuda Reef. As to why Captain Dimitriadis elected to make a night approach to the island without a proper chart when there was no pressing need, no explanation was offered to the court of inquiry.

Some months before the *Tifoso* landed the fortuitous charter and seemed condemned to lie rusting in Boston for ever, insurance was taken out on her hull for a total of $43 million. It was later estimated that her market value was no more than $7 million. On that dark, stormy night when she found the Great Bermuda Reef with such uncanny accuracy, the *Tifoso* was therefore over-insured to the tune of $36 million. The underwriters paid up without a murmur of dissent.

23 Beware the English Channel!

The English Channel has long been known for its extremes of weather. Facing south-west, it is like a huge, gaping mouth into which, from time to time, rushed all the pent-up fury of the North Atlantic. In winter, Storm Force 10 is par for the course; summer is slightly less malevolent, but any easing of the wind is sure to bring down a blanket of dense fog on these tortuous waters. Over 2,000 wrecks litter this 350-mile-long navigator's nightmare, bearing witness to the folly of those who dared to underestimate the perils of the Channel.

On the night of 22 January 1984 the English Channel was in an ugly mood. Storm-force winds, whipped up by a deep depression passing to the north of Scotland, were building up, bringing with them very high seas and driving rain. It was not a night for the unwary to be abroad.

One such was the 2,997-ton, Liberian-flag motor ship *Radiant Med*, which at midnight was off Alderney and clawing her way down Channel in the teeth of the wind. The 14-year-old *Radiant Med*, loaded with 5,000 tons of bulk grain and bound for the Congo, was entered in Lloyd's Shipping Index as owned by Maritime Star Shipping Ltd of Monrovia and managed by Middle East Agents Ltd of Piraeus, Greece. She carried a total crew of twenty-five, of which her officers were Indian and her ratings Filipino. Her master, Captain A. D'Souza, and her chief officer, Subhas Singh Tanwar, both held Liberian masters' certificates, issued on the strength of their Indian certificates.

For a small ship, deep loaded and facing a passage of 4,800 miles, during which she would be exposed to the full rigours of the North Atlantic in winter, the *Radiant Med* had one dangerous weakness – a weakness that was to be aggravated by a serious underestimation of the power of the sea. Unlike that of modern ships, which have tight-fitting, hydraulically controlled, steel hatch-covers, the watertight integrity of her two cargo holds was dependent on light steel pontoons, over which were stretched canvas tarpaulins. The whole was designed to be kept firmly in place by steel locking-bars fitted athwartships, one bar securing each section of pontoons. Under the International Load Line Regulations, this was considered to be a watertight closure. Unfortunately, over the years many of the *Radiant Med*'s hatch locking-bars had gone missing, and those still on board could not be correctly fitted, due to alterations recently made to the hatch coamings. As a substitute for the bars, D'Souza had concluded that rope nets, stretched over the hatch tarpaulins and lashed down to the deck, would do just as well. While this expedient might have held good in more benign waters, in the Western Approaches in winter it was tempting providence.

When a reluctant daylight came on the 23rd, the *Radiant Med* was thirty miles west of Guernsey and determinedly attempting to punch her way through mountainous seas. As water is incompressible, she was making little progress. In refusing to reduce speed, Captain D'Souza was ignoring one of the basic rules of good seamanship and punishing his ship needlessly. This he was to regret.

The wind had veered more to the west and was gusting Force 11 when, at 16.00 that day, Chief Officer Tanwar took over the watch on the bridge. The *Radiant Med*'s engines were still making full revolutions, and she was burying her bows deep in the advancing walls of green water, her propeller racing wildly each time her stern lifted high. The air was full of flying spray, torn from the crests of the tumbling waves, and her decks were constantly awash with foaming water which tugged and plucked with eager fingers at her lightly secured hatches.

At about 17.00 the labouring vessel slammed headlong into a towering wave that had reared up unseen in the darkness, and an avalanche of angry water poured over her bows and thundered the length of her foredeck. To a horrified Tanwar, watching with his face pressed to the glass of the wheelhouse windows, it seemed that the ship would never rise again. But rise she did, shouldering aside the sea with a determination born of desperation.

When the welter of tumbling foam had drained from the

deck, Tanwar saw that the forward derrick of No.2 hatch had been torn from its stowage position. The long steel boom, suspended from the mast by its topping wires, was scything menacingly across the top of the hatch in an ever-increasing arc.

In response to Tanwar's urgent call, D'Souza came to the bridge a few minutes later and quickly grasped the danger of the situation. The rampaging derrick was to some extent restrained by its heavy lifting-tackle, which was lashed to a wooden pallet on the hatch-top. Should this tackle break free, the derrick and its attendant blocks would embark on an orgy of destruction, smashing everything in its path. Most vulnerable – and D'Souza realized this with fear in his heart – were the securing nets and canvas tarpaulins of the hatch-top.

D'Souza now took the only course of action open to him. He brought the ship around until she was stern-on to the seas and ordered the chief officer to take a party of men on deck to secure the derrick. This was really an impossible task, for, even with the vessel's stern to the weather, huge seas were still sweeping her decks. Tanwar and his men were forced to withdraw, but not before they had seen that the heavy derrick tackle was already on the move and tearing the tarpaulins of No.2 hatch to shreds. With no locking-bars in place, it would be only a matter of time before the pounding seas dislodged one or more of the steel pontoons, leaving the hold open to the sea. When he was given this news, D'Souza decided to continue on his present course and run for shelter further up Channel. Unfortunately the nearest refuge from this storm was 120 miles away, on the eastern side of the Cherbourg peninsula.

At first the *Radiant Med* made good progress to the north-east. With the wind and sea astern, she had ceased to pitch heavily, but her decks were still awash at times. She was taking in some water in her forward hold, but the pumps were able to cope. For a while it seemed that the danger might be over. Then, late that night, the situation changed dramatically for the worse. A big wave climbed aboard and swept a pontoon hatch over the side. The sea began to pour into No.2 hold.

D'Souza's 'Mayday' was answered by the French Navy frigate *Casabianca*, which was providentially only fifteen miles or so to the west of the stricken ship. The commander of the *Casabianca* assumed on-the-spot control of the rescue operation, under the direction of the Search and Rescue Centre at Cap de la Hague.

Also listening in was St Peter Port Radio, which prudently alerted the Guernsey lifeboat.

News that the French Navy was close by brought some comfort to those on board the *Radiant Med*, but the position of the ship was deteriorating rapidly. The wind had shifted to the north-west and was gusting to seventy knots, with thirty-five-foot waves racing up astern, each one threatening to overwhelm the small ship. A second pontoon was washed away, and very soon the pumps were fighting a losing battle against the water pouring into the open hatchway of No.2 hold. D'Souza ordered his crew to swing out the lifeboats. In the midst of this frenzied operation the second assistant engineer suffered a heart attack and died. The first act of the tragedy of the night of 23 January had opened.

Shortly before midnight, *Casabianca* was sighted from the bridge of the *Radiant Med*. The frigate was eight miles astern and battling her way towards the Liberian ship, which was now making four knots to the north-east. Conditions were such that there was no question of *Casabianca*'s lowering a boat, but a helicopter was reported to be on the way from the French mainland. From now on, it would clearly be a race against time, for the *Radiant Med* was becoming more and more sluggish in her movements, less willing to rise each time the sea pressed her down.

D'Souza, fearful that his ship did not have long to live, now requested the frigate to close up and make an attempt to take off the *Radiant Med*'s crew. *Casabianca* was reluctant to do so. Her commander suggested that D'Souza increase speed, with the object of making Cherbourg as soon as possible or, if that failed, beach his ship to the west of the port. The *Radiant Med* was at that time twenty miles west-south-west of Guernsey, and steering to pass to the south of the island. Despite the grave risk they knew they were taking, the ship's chief and third engineers went below and increased speed to ten knots.

At 00.52 on the 24th came the bitter news that the helicopter, unable to cope with the extreme weather, had turned back. Ten minutes later the *Radiant Med*'s steering-gear failed and the ship's head fell off until she was beam-on to the sea and rolling helplessly in the trough. D'Souza decided that the time had come to abandon ship. He called *Casabianca*, now only two miles off, and asked her to stand by to pick them up.

Due to the water in her hold, the ship now had a heavy list to port, and it proved impossible to lower the starboard lifeboat. Likewise the port lifeboat became jammed in its davits and refused to budge. The inflatable liferaft was launched but, in the confusion of the night, it floated away before anyone could board. At that point the ship began to sink under them, and D'Souza and his men had no alternative but to throw themselves on the mercy of the sea.

D'Souza and Tanwar led the way over the side, hurling themselves into the churning sea, their bodies recoiling with shock as they hit the icy water. When Tanwar came to the surface, he saw that one of the *Radiant Med*'s lifeboats had released itself and was floating close to the sinking ship. He struck out and, after a struggle that all but exhausted him, reached the boat and hauled himself over the gunwale. Four other survivors were already in the boat.

Tanwar's relief was short-lived, for no sooner had he collapsed on the bottom boards than the *Radiant Med* rolled over, and her after radio mast crashed down on the lifeboat, causing serious damage. Very soon the boat was waterlogged and floating only on its buoyancy tanks.

Fortunately for those of the Liberian ship's crew who were still alive, St Peter Port Radio had been monitoring the emergency from the start. When it became apparent that the *Radiant Med* was sinking and that *Casabianca* was powerless to help, St Peter Port's harbourmaster took it upon himself to call out the Guernsey lifeboat.

Driving into the teeth of a fifty-knot wind, with very high seas and visibility curtailed by rain, the fifty-two-foot Arun Class lifeboat *Sir William Arnold*, with Coxswain Scales at the helm, made good speed and by 03.00 had *Casabianca* in sight. The frigate was hove-to about one mile from the spot where the *Radiant Med* had gone down, and had the waterlogged lifeboat in the beam of her searchlight. Coxswain Scales brought the *Sir William Arnold* to windward of the boat, and his men went on deck with their safety lines rigged. In a display of superb seamanship and outstanding courage, the RNLI men snatched Chief Officer Tanwar and eight other half-drowned souls from the grip of the sea.

An extensive search was carried out by other ships and RAF Sea King helicopters, but no more survivors were found. Later the bodies of Captain D'Souza and fifteen of his men were picked up. At the inquest held in Guernsey, a pathologist stated that all these men had died by drowning within twenty minutes of entering the water, despite being buoyed up by lifejackets. It was assumed that, already in a state of shock and with their legs acting as involuntary sea anchors, they had drifted face to the wind and had been slowly choked to death by the remorseless seas breaking over their heads.

In the end, it may be said that the *Radiant Med* was a victim of the English Channel in its angriest mood. Yet she need not have been lost. Smaller ships have survived by riding out such a storm, hove-to with the wind and sea on the bow. It was D'Souza's insistence on pressing ahead at full speed in the face of the very severe weather that caused the damage, which eventually led to her loss. With regard to the missing hatch locking-bars, this was also D'Souza's responsibility. As master of the ship, he should have insisted that they were supplied and fitted before sailing. But who knows what pressure he was under from those who employed him? The *Radiant Med* was owned by faceless men of indeterminate nationality, registered in Liberia as a matter of economic expediency and managed in a country in which safety takes second place to productivity. She was just another typical example of the prostitution of a flag for profit.

24   A Large Naval Target

The sun hoisted itself slowly over the eastern horizon, turning the unruffled waters of the Persian Gulf from the sombre grey of night to an opaline blue. A shoal of tiny, irridescent flying fish whirled into silent flight from the cool depths, while a lone dolphin saluted the new day with a lazy arch of its back that barely rippled the surface of the sea.

On the bridge of the 236,000-tonne Liberian-flat tanker *Caribbean Breeze*, Captain David McCaffrey, tired and unshaven, winced as the rising sun struck fire from the wheelhouse windows. Silently he cursed the malfunctioning boiler which had reduced his ship's speed to a mere eleven knots during the night. As a result of this, the 1,100-foot-long tanker, her white-painted bridge structure towering seventy feet above the waterline, was now in a very exposed position, etched in bold relief against an empty sea and sky.

Some thirty-six hours earlier, the *Caribbean Breeze* had slipped clear of her berth at Mina Al Ahmadi after loading a cargo of 1.8 million barrels of Kuwaiti crude oil. She was drawing sixty-eight feet and at the best of times her two-day passage through the shallow waters of the Gulf would have been hazardous. Now that the Iran/Iraq conflict, bogged down in a dreadful war of attrition ashore, had spilled over into the sea lanes in earnest, the risks faced by a loaded tanker were awesome. It was March 1985, and in the previous twelve months the Persian Gulf had been the scene of vicious attacks on no fewer than sixty-seven merchant ships, most of them large tankers like the *Caribbean Breeze*. Iraq, desperate to cut off the flow of Iran's oil exports, was flinging Exocet missiles at everything that moved in the vicinity of the beleaguered Kharg Island, while Iran, adopting a grim 'ship-for-ship' policy, was relentlessly deploying her Phantom aircraft, armed with

American Maverick missiles, against ships carrying Kuwaiti and
Saudi Arabian oil out of the Gulf. Both sides were making war
on neutral ships with impunity.

David McCaffrey, 54-year-old British master of the
Caribbean Breeze, rasped the bristles of his unshaven chin and
reflected on the circumstances which had dragged him into this
crazy war. Until two years before, all his working life had been
spent in British ships, starting as a young cadet with the
prestigious Blue Funnel Line in 1946. When he had first put up
his four gold rings of command, the future had looked secure.
Then, when Britain's merchant fleet collapsed under the weight
of cut-price foreign competition, like thousands of other British
masters and officers he had been forced to 'go foreign' to keep
the pay-cheques coming in. He had little dreamed that he would
end up in command of a Kuwaiti-owned, Liberian-registered
supertanker, a prime target for Iranian missiles, slinking through
the night like a hunted animal and hiding in friendly waters by
day.

On that fine Sunday morning in March, 1985, the *Caribbean
Breeze* was approaching a 'safe' anchorage twelve miles north of
the lonely Halul Island, which lies on the edge of the Great
Pearl Bank and just inside the territorial waters of Qatar. There
she would seek sanctuary for the day, before making the final
dash for the Straits of Hormuz and the open sea.

At twenty miles off the island, McCaffrey eased his engines
down to the minimum revolutions compatible with steerage-
way. The tremendous momentum the 237,000 tonner had built
up while steaming through the night would be sufficient to carry
her into the anchorage. With the 200-foot-high lump of barren
rock that was Halul showing clearly on the radar screen,
McCaffrey moved out into the wing of the bridge and scanned
the horizon with his binoculars, feeling the tension slowly
draining away. Then a tiny black silhouette appeared low down
in the eastern sky and he froze.

The aircraft swept in and began to circle the *Caribbean Breeze*
as she coasted through the water. McCaffrey's knuckles were
white as he adjusted the focus of his powerful 10x50s. The
visitor was a large, four-engined plane, similar to the old British
Viscount, but the Iranian markings were unmistakeable.

Following the big aircraft round as it circled persistently,
McCaffrey experienced anger, frustration and, momentarily,

fear. The pattern was only too familiar. This was the spotter plane, sent out to make the identification. Even now his ship's name and particulars were being radioed back to base on the Iranian coast, where it would be quickly established that the *Caribbean Breeze* was carrying Kuwaiti oil and therefore in the service of an enemy of Iran. The neutral Liberian flag would be ignored, and the scrambling of a missile-carrying Phantom would follow.

McCaffrey lowered his binoculars and pondered his next move. Had he been in one of Blue Funnel's twenty-one-knot cargo ships, his course of action would have been clear – a quick dash for the safety of Qatari inshore waters. Unfortunately the *Caribbean Breeze* was no clipper-bowed ocean greyhound. Her maximum speed when loaded was twelve knots and it would take her engineers several hours to work up to that. She was also drawing over eleven fathoms of water, and to take her close into the coast would be to court disaster. There could be no running away.

Swallowing hard, McCaffrey re-entered the wheelhouse and reached for the VHF. He first called Bahrain, where two US frigates were based, reported that his ship appeared to be in imminent danger of attack and asked for help. 'Sorry,' the reply came back, 'we can do nothing until you are actually hit.' Shaking his head in disbelief, McCaffrey next contacted the port of Doha, only forty miles away and the base of a small but powerful Qatari naval force. The reply from Doha was substantially the same. The *Caribbean Breeze* was apparently nobody's problem until she became a casualty.

McCaffrey was now left with only one alternative: he must take his ship into Qatari territorial waters off Halul Island as quickly as possible. There she might be safe from attack. But a 237,000-ton tanker has no brakes and, without the aid of tugs, can be brought to a halt only by gradually shedding her vast momentum. He dare not increase speed for fear of overruning the anchorage and ending up in shallow water.

Another hour passed, with the *Caribbean Breeze* creeping in towards her anchorage, all the while being circled by her unwelcome escort. On the bridge, the tension was mounting. McCaffrey paced the port wing, occasionally entering the wheelhouse to give quiet helm and engine orders. At the chart table, Second Officer Jaffrey maintained a meticulous plot, while Third Officer Finnbar O'Driscoll manned the radar. The Filipino helmsman kept his eyes glued to the clicking gyro compass.

At 7.30 the big, four-engined aircraft suddenly broke off its patient surveillance and roared away to the east. McCaffrey knew that the run-up to the attack on his ship was under way.

The wait was long and agonizing, the giant tanker inching her way towards sanctuary, the muted thump of her idling engines the only sound on the still morning air. At 08.00 Chief Officer Stephen Mitchell began the long walk up the exposed foredeck to his anchor station in the bows. The hot sun blazed down out of a cloudless sky, but the sweat soaking Mitchell's thin tropical shirt was ice-cold.

At 08.30 the *Caribbean Breeze* was fifteen miles to the north of Halul Island and only three miles outside Qatari territorial waters. McCaffrey's hopes were now rising. Perhaps the attack would not come after all and, as on any normal morning, he would soon be enjoying breakfast in the officers' saloon below the bridge. Then, as he walked from the port wing into the wheelhouse, his tired brain reviving at the thought of sizzling bacon and eggs, he heard Second Officer Jaffrey's sharp cry of warning.

The Iranian jet came screaming in out of the sun, an ominous black shape detaching itself from beneath the wings before the plane swept skywards again. Seconds later the 645 lb guided missile crashed into the tall bridge structure of the *Caribbean Breeze* and exploded with a deafening roar. Before the world went black, McCaffrey saw the armoured glass of the wheelhouse windows shatter like thin ice under a hammer and felt a searing pain in his left arm.

When he regained his senses, McCaffrey struggled to his feet and looked around in horror. The wheelhouse, with all its sophisticated equipment, was now a tangled mass of twisted wreckage. A few feet away from where he had fallen, the steel deck had been peeled back by a giant hand, and smoke and flames were pouring up from below. Ugly shards of glass lay everywhere.

McCaffrey's first thought was for his men. Fighting his way through the smoke and wreckage, he found the Filipino helmsman propped up against the after bulkhead, where he had been thrown by the force of the explosion. The man was moaning but not badly injured. Second Officer Jaffrey was on his knees near the chart table, his hands clasped to his face, blood running through his fingers. He had been blinded by flying glass. Third Officer O'Driscoll, although dazed and cut, was still on his feet and already searching in the wreckage for the first aid box. It was only when he felt a terrible weakness creeping over him that McCaffrey realized that his white uniform was turning scarlet with the blood spurting from a severed artery in his left arm. He was barely conscious when O'Driscoll applied the life-saving tourniquet.

The missile had hit directly below the tanker's wheelhouse, creating a blackened shell out of the once luxuriously appointed owner's suite. The adjoining radio-room was a smoking shambles, and fire was sweeping through the accommodation. All communications between the bridge and engine-room had been cut.

The *Caribbean Breeze*, her engines still turning and with her bridge and its occupants temporarily out of action, continued to slide relentlessly through the water. If the fire in her accommodation did not first ignite the gas given off by her cargo, causing a cataclysmic explosion, she would surely pile up on the reefs of Halul Island.

McCaffrey, the flow of blood from his shattered arm partially stemmed, moved swiftly and decisively. He dispatched a messenger to the engine-room with the order to stop the engines and, when this was done, sent word forward to Mitchell to let go both anchors.

A cloud of red dust erupted from the forecastle head as the cables rattled out through the hawsepipes, and slowly, with the flukes of her huge, high-tensile steel anchors scoring deep furrows in the sea bed, the *Caribbean Breeze* reluctantly came to a halt. McCaffrey then went below to organize the fire-fighting operation.

It was almost two hours after the attack before a helicopter of the Qatari Air Force arrived in response to the 'Mayday' calls sent out by the damaged tanker's radio officer. By this time McCaffrey and his team had succeeded in extinguishing the fire in the accommodation. The captain was now weak from loss of blood, but only when he was satisfied that his ship was safe did he hand over command to Mitchell and allow himself to be flown to hospital with the other injured men. The *Caribbean*

Breeze was later taken in tow by salvage tugs and anchored off Dubai for repairs. Two months later she was back in service.

There can be no doubt that Captain David McCaffrey, by his courageous action and impeccable leadership, saved the *Caribbean Breeze* from total destruction, thereby averting a loss to her owners of in excess of $60 million US. He also avoided massive and widespread pollution of Qatari waters. One would have expected recognition and reward to follow swiftly. This was not to be. At the time of writing, David McCaffrey, partly disabled by his injuries, his career as a ship-master finished, was still engaged in a prolonged legal battle with his former Kuwaiti employers for adequate financial compensation. It is a battle in which he has precious few allies. Such are the rewards of seafaring in the 1980s.

Glossary

Abaft: Behind in relation to something on the ship.

Abeam: At right angles to the fore and aft line of the ship.

Able seaman: A first-class or certificated seaman.

Afterdeck: That part of the maindeck abaft the bridge.

Amidships: The middle part of the ship.

Astern: Behind the ship.

Athwartships: Across the beam of the ship.

Barque: Three-masted sailing vessel square-rigged on the fore and main masts and fore-and-aft rigged on the mizen mast.

Beam: Width of the vessel at her widest part.

Binnacle: Pedastal supporting ship's compass.

Boatswain: Senior deck rating.

Bower anchor: Main anchor stowed in bows of ship.

Bowsprit: Spar projecting forward from the bows, which enables ship to carry more sail.

Breeches buoy: Life-saving apparatus using hawser set up between shore and ship, from which lifebuoy is suspended to carry survivors ashore.

Broach to: To swing beam on to wind and sea.

Bulkhead: Steel or wooden division beween two compartments.

Bulwark: Shield or fence around open deck of vessel to prevent persons or goods falling or being washed overboard.

Cant: To turn on an axis.

Clipper: Fast sailing-ship built for speed rather than cargo-carrying capacity.

Clipper bow: Raked bow as on clipper ship.

Clutter: Interference on radar screen caused by waves or precipitation.

Coaming: Steel parapet around a hatchway.

Collier: Small ship used exclusively for the carriage of coal.

Conning (the ship): Directing the course to be steered.

Crankcase: Casing surrounding crankshaft of ship's main engine.

Crow's nest: Look-out platform situated high on the forward mast.

Cruiser stern: Sloping stern similar to that of naval ship of same name.

Davit pin: Pin securing lifeboat davits while at sea.

Deadweight: Maximum weight of cargo, bunkers, fresh water and stores that can be carried by a ship.

Deck house: Structure built on deck for stores.

Deck plating: Plates of steel deck.

Derrick: Boom used for loading and discharging cargo.

Displacement: The weight of water displaced by a vessel.

Dog's leg: Crooked or bent.

Doldrums: Area of light wind and calms near the Equator.

Donkeyman: Senior engine-room rating.

Double bottom: Space between bottom of ship's hull and water-tight floor of holds. Used for ballast water or fuel oil.

E.T.A.: Estimated time of arrival.

Fathom: Six feet or 1.82 metres.

Fine (on bow): Up to about five degrees of arc.

Flag of convenience: Flag which allows registry of foreign ships to avoid irksome legal or financial restraints in country of ownership.

Fluke: The hooked part of an anchor.

Flush deck: Deck running from forward to aft without interruption of forecastle or poop.

Flying bridge: Open navigation bridge.

Forecastle: Space below deck in the bows of the ship used for crew accommodation or stores.

Forecastle head: Deck above forecastle.

Fore deck: That part of the main deck forward of the bridge.

Forepeak: Ballast or freshwater tank in bows of ship.

Freeboard: Distance from main deck to the waterline.

Gale force (8); wind speed 34 – 40 knots)39 – 46 m.p.h.).

Gig: Small open boat.

Gunwale: Point where the hull joins the weather deck.

Halyard: Light rope for hoisting flags.

Hatch board: Portable wooden cover for hatchway.

Hatchway: Opening in deck usually giving access to cargo hold.

Hawsepipe: Pipe through which anchor cable passes.

Hawser: Heavy wire or rope.

Heave to: To stop the ship at sea.

Hurricane force (12): Wind speed 64 knots (74 m.p.h.) and over.

In ballast: Without cargo.

Knot: One nautical mile per hour, a nautical mile being 6080 feet or the length of one minute of latitude at the Equator.

Larboard: Old name for port or left-hand side of ship when facing forward.

Lead: Weight attached to line used to determine the depth of the water.

Leadsman: A seaman who casts the lead.

Lee: The sheltered side.

Lee shore: A shore upon which the wind blows.

Lloyd's register: Body which lays down the rules regarding the building and maintenance of ships.

Main deck: The principal deck on a vessel having more than one deck.

Man-of-war: Armed naval ship.

Master: In command of a merchant ship.

Mayday: Distress code word used on radio telephone meaning 'I require immediate assistance.'

OBO: Oil/bulk/ore carrier. Large ship built to carry oil or bulk cargo (grain, ores, etc.).

Ordinary seaman: Uncertificated seaman with at least twelve months' sea service.

Packet: Small passenger or mail ship.

Paddle-box: Casing covering paddle wheels.

Plimsoll line: Line painted on side of ship indicating the maximum depth to which she may legally load.

Point (of compass): 11¼ degrees of arc.

Pontoon: Portable hollow steel slab for closing cargo hatchway.

Poop: Raised deck at after end of ship.

Pooped: To be overtaken and swamped by wave coming up astern.

Port: Left-hand side of the ship when facing forward.

Put about: To turn back.

Quarter: That part of the ship which is halfway between the beam and stern.

Roaring forties: Belt of strong westerly winds in South Indian Ocean between latitudes of 40°S and 50°S.

Schooner: Two-masted sailing ship rigged fore and aft but with square topsails on the foremast.

Scupper: Drain at ship's side and in holds to carry away excess water.

Shellback: A seaman of long experience. Usually with reference to sail.

Shelter deck: Deck below the main deck running the length of the ship without dividing bulkheads.

Slab-sided: Straight-sided.

Sloop: Small naval vessel used mainly for auxiliary purposes.

Starboard: Right-hand side of the ship when facing forward.

Stator: Stationary part of generator.

Steerage: Communal third-class passenger accommodation below decks.

Steerage way: The minimum speed at which a ship's rudder will have effect.

Stern bar: Post at stern of ship to which rudder is attached.

Stokehold: That part of the engine-room where the boiler furnaces are situated.

Storm force (10): Wind speed 48 – 55 knots (55 – 63 m.p.h.).

Tonne: Metric ton of 1000 kilograms. It is customary to quote the tonnage of oil tankers in tonnes.

Torque: Twisting motion of force.

Trade winds: Winds between 30°N and 30°S of Equator which blow consistently from one direction.

Trimmed down: Partly ballasted and low in the water.

Trimmer: Engine-room rating who supplies firemen with coal.

Trinity house: Body responsible for manning and upkeep of lighthouses, lightships and buoys in the coastal waters of England, Wales and the Channel Islands.

Trough: The hollow between the crests of two waves.

Tween deck: Usually first deck below the main deck.

VLCC: Very Large Crude Carrier. Usually oil tanker of about 300,000 tonnes deadweight and upwards.

Wear ship: To put the vessel onto another tack by first bringing the wind astern.

Weather deck: The deck open to the weather.

Well deck: Space on the main deck either between raised forecastle and bridge or between poop and bridge.

Windjammer: Large square-rigged sailing ship.

100 A1: Highest classification at Lloyd's.

Index